The Montrose line is descended from The Great Marquis of
Montrose who was sentenced to death in 1650 by the Scottish
Parliament for his services to the cause of King Charles II.

The Hamilton line is descended from King James II

Duke of Montrose (Peerage of Scotland 1707)
d. 1742

James, 3rd Marquis of Hamilton, created Duke of Hamilton
in 1643. d. 1649

William, 2nd Duke of Montrose
d. 1790

William, 2nd Duke of Hamilton
d. 1651

James, 3rd Duke of Montrose
d. 1836

Anne (Good Duchess Anne) m. William, 1st Earl of Selkirk, created
d. 1716   3rd Duke of Hamilton in 1660

James, 4th Duke of Montrose m. Caroline Agnes, dau. of
d. 1874   2nd Baron Decies

James, 4th Duke of Hamilton
d. 1712

James, 5th Duke of Hamilton
d. 1743

Douglas, 5th Duke of Montrose m. Violet Hermione, dau. of
d. 1925   Sir Frederick Ulrick Graham

James, 6th Duke of Hamilton
d. 1758

James, 7th Duke of Hamilton
d. 1769

Douglas, 8th Duke of Hamilton
d. 1799

Archibald, 9th Duke of Hamilton
d. 1819

Alexander, 10th Duke of Hamilton m. Susan Beckford, dau. of
d. 1852   William Beckford

William, 11th Duke of Hamilton m. Princess Marie of Baden
d. 1863

†William, 12th Duke of Hamilton m. Mary Montagu, dau. of
d. 1895   Duke of Manchester

Mary Louise Hamilton (only child of 12th Duke)
d. 1957

†The sister of the 12th Duke of Hamilton, Lady Mary,
married, firstly, Prince Albert of Monaco.

Never behind

Forget not

James, 6th Duke of Montrose — m. — Mary Louise Hamilton
d. 1954

(Lady) Mary   (Lord) Ronald, d. 1978   (Lady) Jean

Angus, 7th Duke of Montrose

This book is dedicated to my son

CHARLES

as a reminder that the old
were once very young

The Authoress

CASTLES IN THE AIR

by

Lady Jean Fforde

*The memories of a childhood
in two castles*

STUART TITLES LTD

Paperback Edition 1996
published by
STUART TITLES LTD
268 Bath Street, Glasgow G2 4JR

ISBN 0 948474 15 7

First published in 1982 by Kilbrannan Publishing Ltd
Paperback (revised) edition 1996 by Stuart Titles Ltd

Production and printing by D-Zine, 268 Bath Street, Glasgow G2 4JR
Revised typesetting and cover by Cliff M.
Photographs reproduced by J. Stedman, Arran AV Photography
Binding by Mitchell & Moreland Ltd, 48 King Street, Glasgow G1 5QX

CONTENTS

ILLUSTRATIONS

Page

ACKNOWLEDGEMENTS

In the first place I must record my indebtedness to the well-known Scottish authoress, Lavinia Derwent, who first sowed the seeds of this book in my mind. Secondly to Mr. & Mrs. Richard Hough who took time and trouble to really give helpful suggestions to me — even if it was to tear up the first effort and start again! Thirdly to Eva Marsden who, with great good humour, typed and re-typed the manuscript many times without showing any desperation and who, in fact, has encouraged me at all times. What could be more fitting than that it is the first book that her newly-formed Kilbrannan Publishing Company should produce. If it is any help in starting a new industry on the Isle of Arran then that will be a great reward to us. Fourthly, I must mention that the photographs were taken and, in many cases, developed by my late mother, the Duchess of Montrose.

PREFACE

In order to understand more fully the family Montrose who lived for six months at Brodick and six months at Buchanan, perhaps a little explanation is necessary.

My mother, born Lady Mary Douglas Hamilton, was the only child of the twelfth Duke of Hamilton who owned the whole of the Isle of Arran as well as Hamilton Palace in Lanarkshire, Easton Park in Suffolk, a house in Paris and a house in London.

He died when my mother was ten years old, and Arran and Easton were placed in a Trust for her use for life.

She married my Father the sixth Duke of Montrose who owned Buchanan Castle, the east side of Loch Lomond to Inversnaid, Loch Katrine, Aberfoyle; and, in a line back to Drymen and Mugdock (near Glasgow).

Both Mother and Father were crippled by Death Duties when they were introduced, not to mention racing debts from ancestors on both sides of the family.

They married in 1905, and a blissfully happy marriage it was. They weathered the storms of two World Wars and the Great Depression; but suffered from bad advice, and dishonesty among the advisers.

Both were deeply Christian in their beliefs and were highly respected and loved by those on their estates and those who worked for them.

My Father's deafness and my Mother's shyness stopped them from a social life, which meant that as children we led a lonely life.

Father was an inventor, usually before his time, which was nice for everybody except the Bank Manager and the Accountant.

In his youth he managed to get the Board of Trade to agree that sailing ships should not be sent to sea without an agreed tonnage of ballast after dropping their cargo; also that the number of crew would reflect the square footage of canvas (sailing ships foundered because of crew exhaustion more often than through inadequacy of the ship).

Around the time of the Boer War he was trying (with one of the Guinnesses) to start the RNVR. They succeeded just before World War I, and my father said his proudest day was when he became enrolment No. 1 in the RNVR.

In 1925 Father was instrumental in the separation of the Scottish Royal National Lifeboat Institution from the RNLI of Great Britain, as he felt this would increase both morale and income. He was proved right on both counts.

I won't bore you with his "smokeless fuel" endeavours which cost thousands of pounds, but it may be of interest that it was thanks to his efforts that hearing aids were made available through the National Health. Father, who was Chairman of the Deaf Institute of Great Britain, insisted that these should be of the very latest type, which he had seen and enquired about in the USA.

A keen fighter for Devolution, he joined the Liberal Party as he felt they were more sympathetic to his beliefs. With deafness such as his, he could not take meetings without the help of someone to note down the questions asked of him. This usually was J.M. Bannerman, later a Liberal Lord, whose daughter Mrs Michie has been Liberal MP for Argyll for some years now.

My Mother, like her Mother before her, was a great horsewoman and an extremely knowledgeable gardener. A good musician, she studied the history of opera in Vienna and played the violin and piano. She won a gold medal for drawing, and was very good at sculpture; several of her bronzes are still with members of her family.

Had she needed to earn a living, she would have been a nurse. In the First World War she became Theatre Sister in Bellahouston Hospital, Glasgow. Mother was a good shot, and maintained that had she not owned one of the greatest sporting estates in Britain, her hobby would have been poaching!

My parents had four children. The older son, to their sadness, left home to work and live in Rhodesia. My sister Mary married young. My second brother firstly lived in South Africa and then in Jamaica. I was the youngest by eight years. Largely because of this gap, and being born so soon after World War I when social life was eclipsed for many years, I had a very lonely life. By then the Estate in Suffolk had been sold, also the houses in Paris and London. Few of my parents' friends journeyed north to be with them, despite the fact that travelling in those days was more comfortable than today!

1

TRAVELLING PEOPLE A LA 1923

HEN the wild geese left and the sheets of daffodils came out in the Buchanan woods I knew it was time to return to Brodick. The great packing started again.

Children pick up the atmosphere from grown ups, and the days of packing and days of arrangements gave a certain amount of electricity to the air. Nanny busied around — for all journeys clean clothes had to be worn "in case there was an accident, what would the doctors think if you did not have clean clothes on?"

Nanny's packing was further complicated by Mother's gift to her of a crystal set wireless. Each part had to be padded with cotton wool and tissue paper then placed in an oversized box. Wherever I moved in the nursery there would be a shout,

"Watch out, clumsy, watch out for my wireless!"

Eventually the precious box containing the crystal set would travel carefully on someone's knee on the bus hired to take the staff to the pier at Ardrossan, because there was not room for it in the Studebaker with us.

A cattle float, hired for the luggage, followed the convoy — rather coming down in the world after the special trains and the through carriages in which the family had moved about in the more flush days.

It was always exciting driving through the Spring morning to Ardrossan over Erskine Ferry. In those days the ferry took about a dozen cars and ran on chains, one on each side. If the Clyde was busy with passing ships we would have to sit and

wait till they had passed which could easily be half an hour.

We always arrived in good time for the boat because Mother suffered from train fever, and Tommy Watson, the chauffeur, suffered from pessimism and was sure that each tyre in turn would have a puncture if nothing worse went wrong with the car. Nanny, of course, suffered from knowing she would be sea sick. Usually we got to Winton Pier, Ardrossan, with hours to spare.

The boat was small, capable of taking only a few cars, and there were no big lorries carried then, so there were no long queues. To load a car, two wooden planks were placed by the crew in front of the wheels of the car on the pier and propped up against the deck of the boat. If the tide was high the angle could be most alarming and blocks were used on the ship to make as gentle an angle as possible. Try as they would a car often got the undercarriage stuck and men had to heave and lift, and heave and shout instructions. Chocks were pushed under the pier end of the planks to raise them, more under the boat end to lessen the angle still more. Most drivers were so scared they would not have known their name if you had asked them, let alone which gear was which. If they looked out of the driver's window they looked right down into the sea. Tommy, like anyone else, was white to the gills.

The driver's troubles were nowhere at an end on reaching the deck. Along the deck and close to the funnel were heavy seats known as Buoyant Appliances, with air tanks beneath them so they could do duty as life rafts if the ship sank, and there were ropes attached for the survivors to cling to at their side. These left a very narrow passage for the drivers to park their cars and often one had to back almost the length of the ship to the bow. Here, too, there was trouble because the only way to transport cattle was to halter them and tie them to the railings. Woe betide anyone with smart shoes who got out of their car in that area of the ship!

They were small ships, low in the water, and could maneouvre into Ardrossan in most weathers. Strict economy had not gripped the nation in those days and it was considered more important to stick to the timetable than to economise in coal. Several of the boats were capable of doing 21 knots and the recognised time from Brodick to Glasgow was 85 minutes by boat and train.

The dining saloon on board had white starched tablecloths and artificial flowers in plated vases. It was fun to go there because it was different from the nursery and to be allowed to choose one's own breakfast or lunch was very grown up and took a lot of thought — bacon and eggs of all kinds, herring, kippers, sausages and so on — what a meal they served, no paper plates and plastic cups in those days.

Of course I only went to the dining room if there was another member of the family to take me because Nanny made up her mind weeks in advance that she was going to be sea sick during the crossing. The roughness of the sea had little or nothing to do with it. Once on deck she would hurry off to a draughty area on the lee side of the boat and wrap herself up in rugs to see the ordeal out with stoicism. If she was not sick I think she was disappointed.

"Lawks alive, child, but I was nearly sick on that terrible boat," she would say.

When she and I were alone on the boat one of the crew members, Mr. McNab (Ned) would look after me. He would take me to see the engines, huge, shining piston rods driving forwards and backwards, their brass bearings glistening, accompanied by the noise of great power. Further back on the same deck was a viewing point where we could watch the paddles driving through the water. From where we watched they turned almost at eye level. Sadly, Mr.McNab died early from cancer without knowing that his son would become Commodore of the fleet of Clyde steamers belonging now to Caledonian MacBrayne, and his daughter was to be one of the first women District Councillors before the new regional government was started, and Commissioner of the Girl Guides for Arran.

There was beautiful wood panelling on all the ships, mahogany, I think, round the dining salon and the first class passenger lounge. The settees were upholstered in red plush and red plush formed the curtains at the entrance.

The Arran piers belonged to the Estate and had to be built and maintained by my mother through the Arran and Easton Trustees. Brodick Pier was half the size it is now, but even so, it cost thousands of pounds to maintain and pier dues of 3d were charged for everyone landing and leaving.

On our return to the island there was a small reception committee on the pier to meet my parents. Mr. Laidlaw, the Factor, in his crottle-coloured tweed plus fours and tweed hat to match. Known locally as "The Great I Am" or just "I" as he was a great user of the first person singular. The Pier Master was there, and last but not least, Wee Geordie McCabe. I believe he started life as a porter at Ardrossan but I had never known a boat to arrive without Geordie being there to catch the bow rope. He was less than five feet tall, walked on his heels with his toes turned out to the side, always the end of a cigarette in his mouth, (somehow I cannot remember a newly-lit cigarette in his mouth), a cloth cap pushed well back from his cheery rubicund face, and a collarless flannel shirt. I saw once in a newspaper that recorded Geordie's retirement that it was reckoned he had consumed about 11,000 gallons of beer and they may have been right because he was very regular in his habits.

As soon as the ropes were tied he seemed to disappear

into thin air till the next boat was due. The Pier Master spoke to him about his habits, my Father spoke to him, he was sent letters of reprimand and letters of warning with no effect, and Geordie's cheerful face met the boat for 41 years till old age finally made him retire. There was a time when the "clack" (gossip) of the village remarked on the abnormal amount of dirty linen the Douglas Hotel was sending away to the laundry. A big wicker hamper was trundled down from the hotel each morning and yesterday's hamper trundled back. If anyone had had the wits to lift the lid Wee Geordie McCabe's cheerful face would have looked up at them from the bottom of the hamper! The hotel porter wheeled him to and fro for years so he should not be seen!

Tommy Watson off-loaded the Studebaker down more slippery planks while we disembarked, and then drove us through the village viewing the wide sandy bay and the hills standing peacefully in the Spring sunshine, and up the long drive to the castle, the neatly trimmed beech hedges just breaking into leaf. At the door of the castle stood the dignified figure of Mr. Allan, the butler, ready to greet us.

The first day at Brodick spelled perfect freedom for me. Everyone was far too busy unpacking and settling in, and they wanted me out of the way.

Down the big staircase I went, out of the front door onto the wide gravel sweep most meticulously raked each morning by one of the gardeners. His raking was the first sound one heard on a summer morning. Two steep banks sloped away down to the azaleas, just bursting with the promise of summer, their buds of reds, pink and yellows of every shade showing up against the dark green of the fir trees, sheets of white narcissus and bluebells among them. At the top of the bank was a little patch of yellow cowslips that Mother had brought with her from her beloved Easton Park to remind her

Brodick Castle

of all her happiness there.

I ran along the lawn to the summer house, heather-thatched and built by the carpenters from fir trees in the round with the bark left on them. It overlooked the walled garden of formal design, with the brilliant colours of tulips and forget-me-nots and wallflowers. Beyond the sea would glitter. Past the summer house and through the wrought iron gates there was a sheet of bluebells, about five acres of them, with cherry trees planted among them, but I preferred to roll down the banks in front of the castle. After all, the grown-ups were too busy today to notice! Nanny forbade it because it stained my knickers green, Mother forbade it because the

banks were steep and long and once started to roll one could not stop and got up a great speed, and she was afraid I would break my neck. I made sure no-one was watching me out of the windows and down I would lie. The grass smelt good at Brodick, it had its own special smell. Then I started rolling over and over, faster and faster. Picking myself up I shook the moss and grass from my hair and clothes. The deed was done, no-one had noticed.

I ran under the five great silver firs, tall and straight as cathedral spires, past the azaleas, though a gate into the rock garden. So many paths — which one could I take? Beautiful species of rhododendrons in every direction, I might go to the lily pond, primulas and mimulus grew along the edge of the stream and round the pond. Oh there! Archie and Bobbie Beaton, the two brothers who always worked side by side and had done so since boyhood and did till they retired years later. A quick word with them — they knew every bird's nest in the garden, and were always cheerful and pleased to see me. Then on to the Bavarian Summer House built for Princess Marie of Baden, my great-grandmother. Octagonal in shape, it had a mosaic of fir-cones on the ceiling and two old murals, one of Brodick Bay and THE THISTLE, my grandfather's yacht, and the other of a castle near Baden-Baden, her home.

The sea lay shimmering below and the fishing boat we had, the dear old CRUBAN was anchored there. I ran on through the woodland garden to find Mr. McGillivray, the head gardener, who would be in his office by the potting shed, or in the vinehouse, or the peach house. Rows of young Spring vegetables were at all stages of growth to keep the castle supplied throughout the summer. Each morning two gardeners carried up large baskets of vegetables and, in the season, melons, peaches, plums, raspberries and strawberries, gooseberries and currants, red and black, both to eat and for jam making.

Mr. McGillivray saw to the day-to-day running of the gardens and was responsible for ordering all that was necessary to keep it in good order, but Mother discussed the seeds to be ordered. She had her own ideas as to which vegetables she liked best and knew exactly what flower seeds she wished. Each summer on a fine day she sat in a chair wearing a large straw hat, scrutinizing a scaled plan of each of the herbaceous borders. Any flower with an offending colour was erased from the plan and the catalogue searched for a different shade or different shape that might improve the overall look. The plans were then given to McGillivray to order the correct seeds. When planting time came the plans were taken to the border and the flowers planted accordingly.

McGillivray guarded his fruit with an ever-watchful eye and I got into some trouble for pinching grapes or peaches. But being my first day back from Buchanan I would get a great welcome, and he would let me have some annual seeds for my little plot of garden up near the castle. The thing I grew best were the most enormous pansies but I have never been able to get them to grow again. The garden was finally taken from me and grassed over as a punishment for bad work in the schoolroom. Bad spelling was the cause, but unfortunately the spelling never improved!

From the kitchen garden I went through a door in the red sandstone wall to the sawmill and into the carpenters' workshop. There were lots of things in the carpenters' shop that would hold the interest of a child for hours. Hanging on the wall were templates for different sized wheels, some for the heavy carts, others for the pony traps or the wagonettes; there were moulds for the cornices of ceilings in the castle and the shooting lodges, keys and locks, nails and hinges, window frames and doors, furniture being mended and new pieces being made. The smell of newly cut wood is good when you run the sawdust through your fingers.

I ran on through the yard to Cladoch to have a quick look at my pony to see if he was all right after the journey from Buchanan, and he whinnied at my coming.

In the last door past the stables was the laundry, reigned over by Mrs. Tommy Watson and her assistants. On washing days a cloud of steam greeted you at the door from the boiler where Mrs. Watson prodded the linen with a paddle like an oar. Round and round she pushed it, then prod, prod, prod and round again. Rinsing took place in wooden sinks along the wall at the side of the room, and then perhaps the hardest work of all was hand-turning the wringer which was very large, as indeed it had to be to take all the linen from the castle as well as the clothes of the whole household. The irons were heated on a grid over a charcoal fire, as were the crimping irons which were used on the wavy edges of the pillow cases and sheets. There was so much activity in the laundry I was always kept at the door in case I went too close to the boilers or the irons.

I crossed the path to the garage where Tommy Watson, her husband, reigned supreme. Tommy Watson had been brought to Scotland from the Easton estate, with his brother, my mother's groom. Both of them had started as stable men. Tommy was known as "Strapper" when he was young and, as the name denoted, he was in charge of saddlery and harnesses. His brother was known as "Brusher" to the end of his days as his job as a boy had been grooming the hunters.

Tommy was put in charge of cars because in the First World War, while in the Army, he had been involved with the development of Britain's secret weapon and had lived for months incarcerated in a barbed wire enclosure until the first

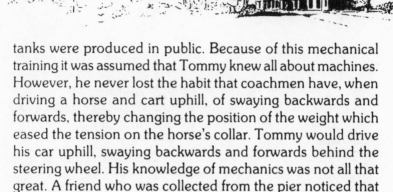

tanks were produced in public. Because of this mechanical training it was assumed that Tommy knew all about machines. However, he never lost the habit that coachmen have, when driving a horse and cart uphill, of swaying backwards and forwards, thereby changing the position of the weight which eased the tension on the horse's collar. Tommy would drive his car uphill, swaying backwards and forwards behind the steering wheel. His knowledge of mechanics was not all that great. A friend who was collected from the pier noticed that he drove in third gear all the way to the castle and asked Tommy if there was something wrong with the car that he had to drive in this one gear.

"Oh no," said Tommy, much offended at a suggestion that his car was wrong, "I've tried all the other gears, but I like this one best."!

No matter what time of day or night, Sundays or weekdays, the cars were brought back to the garage. Tommy would wash them down and rub them just as he would have done had they been horses.

Cladoch was a group of houses which formed the focal point of estate work. As well as the laundry and the carpenters' shop, the electric generators were also situated there. I liked to go down to the Square when the men and their beautiful Clydesdale horses were due to return at tea time bringing home huge wagonloads of timber drawn by two or four Clydesdales. Other men would be sitting astride spare horses with chains and ropes dangling by their sides, the men peacefully smoking their pipes or cigarettes and chatting to each other and whistling. They rode down under a line of horse chestnut trees which bordered the rough road leading to Goatfell and the moors. They took their horses and tied them to the rings inserted in the outside walls of the stables.

Those pulling the timber, first of all took the timber to the sawmill before being unharnessed, and then groomed and brushed in case there was any sand or mud stuck to their backs which would form sores caused by the harness rubbing it into their skins. Their legs were scrubbed down and brushed, and they were dried off before being let loose to drink under the old walnut tree from a sandstone drinking trough about five feet long and two feet deep, cut from one solid piece of sandstone.

The men chatted away, measuring out food and hay, while the horses trotted around in a melee, pushing and shoving each other to get to the water, cantering back across the square to their stables. There would probably be twelve or fifteen of these lovely animals milling around at one time. It was a beautiful sight.

It was nearly tea time and lateness was not allowed so I made my way up the gravel drive or up a short cut through the rhododendrons. The little path I took came out into the sunlight near the castle where my swing hung on the branch of an oak tree. There I could swing to a great height if I worked hard, up and up into the sunlit branches. How I longed to be able to defy the force of gravity and sit up there in the branches and watch the birds all round me and the sunlight peeping through the leaves.

2

ISLE OF ARRAN

Father with Angus, in 1907

IN **May** 1907 when my brother Angus was born, Nanny Breeze moved into the nursery and was to remain as Nanny, friend and confidante to us all until she died in Brodick in 1942. I can only describe her as I knew her about 13 years later. She was a little Shropshire woman, no more than five foot two, quite circular, with a noticeable moustache. In winter she wore a long grey flannel dress, black stockings, black lacing boots (when out of doors), black elastic-sided boots indoors, and a white apron. In summer she wore a white dress that billowed like the sails of the yachts in Brodick Bay. Round her middle was a white starched belt with a silver buckle consisting of two angels kneeling, facing each other, with their wings folded behind them. When we knelt down to

21

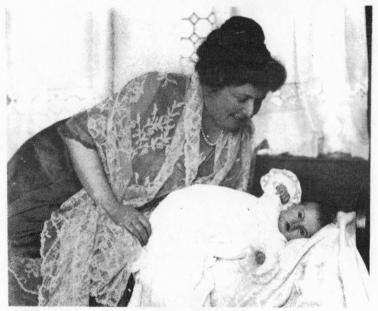

Mother with me, aged five weeks

The motor cycling Duchess! Driving to her shift as a nurse in Lamlash Rehabilitation Hospital

say our prayers at her feet night and morning, she would prompt us on our stumbling way through *Gentle Jesus, meek and mild,* while we tried hard to get our fingers through the buckle between the angels and their wings. How well one remembers the feel and the sounds and the smells of long ago, the feel of the buckle, the sound of the brass handle on the nursery door when it opened and shut, the smell of laundry drying on the black fireguard with its brass top rail in front of the fire, and the smell of the mushrooms we had collected cooking for our nursery tea.

My sister Mary was born two years after Angus and my brother Ronald two years after that. I was mother's "little mistake" as I used to tell her, and she used to be infuriated by this remark.

When the First World War broke out, the social structure of Britain was altered drastically, the old ways were lost and gone for ever. Easton Park, Mother's big estate in Suffolk, was turned into a Red Cross Hospital with my grandmother, the Duchess of Hamilton, as Commandant, and Mother as a V.A.D. Later Mother was transferred to Bellahouston Hospital in Glasgow where she became a Theatre Sister. Father was in Glasgow, too. He was a director of William Beardmore & Co., the shipbuilders, and also a Commodore of the Clyde Division of the R.N.V.R., so Nanny was left in sole charge of the nursery and the nurserymaid which meant that the three toddlers very much looked to her as their friend and confidante, rather than to Mother. It wasn't until Mother returned to Brodick Castle and created a convalescent hospital in The White House in Lamlash that she and her children were reunited; but of course her work took her away from them most of the day. Mother rode from the castle to Lamlash, winter and summer, on the pillion of a motor cycle, which was unusual to say the least, for a woman of that

time. The roads were not tarmacced so it would have been a fairly rough ride.

By the time I was born the family were together and whatever happened, all was well for me: Nanny was in the nursery, Nanny's gnashers (her false teeth) were placed behind the left hand photograph on the marble mantelpiece and the silver buckle on the white starched belt was round her very ample tummy.

Occasionally, Father came to the nursery and said he would bathe me and put me to bed. That was terrific fun. Nanny was left in the day nursery and Father ran the bath. Little or no washing was done, but a splashing match often developed. I was allowed to sit on the back of the bath and shoot down into the water causing such a tidal wave that I flooded the whole bathroom. Then Father would become very contrite and say we should clear up the mess, so down on hands and knees we got, mopping up the water with the bath mat and the towels, making even more of a muddle, but those were nights to remember. I would kneel at his feet to say my prayers even though he could not hear. I remember the feel of his rough kilt (which he always wore in Scotland) against me, the feel of his otter fur sporran on my face, and the smell of his hair lotion. When I got to bed, he would take his gold watch out of his pocket and tell me if I blew on it it would open. I did not see him pressing the little catch at the side, and for a long time I thought my blowing opened it.

If they came home too late for children's hour in the drawing room (bed time was 6.30 p.m.), Mother and Father would come up to say goodnight, all ready for dinner. If there was a house party, and people were there most of the summer, they dressed for dinner. Father's dress kilt was of much lighter material than his day kilt; beautifully fitted and hanging absolutely level. He had Graham tartan silk knitted

stockings, black shoes with silver buckles, a *sgian dubh* of silver with a big cairngorm at the top worn down the side of his stockings, which were kept in place by garters with scarlet flashes protruding from the turn down tops. His evening sporran was whited suede mounted with silver laurel leaves (the badge of the Grahams) and hung on a silver chain round his waist. He wore a yellow or a strawberry coloured shirt with a lace jabot, a Graham tartan waistcoat and Graham tartan jacket with green silk lapels and silver buttons with his crest on them.

However he dressed he was one of the best looking men you could meet. Over six feet tall, he had an aquiline nose and bright blue eyes. The aquiline nose that he, his brother Alastair, and sister Helen had, has been passed down in the family since the Great Marquis of Montrose, King Charles I's famous general, and it occurs in many of the family portraits.

My mother would come to say goodnight in some really lovely dresses, with her long hair piled high on her head, as was the fashion, with tortoiseshell combs holding it and some magnificent jewellery. It is through her family that our problem of weight control has been passed down. It came into the family through my German great-grandmother, Princess Marie of Baden, and has been passed on to all branches of the family. Mother's father died weighing twenty stones. However, Mother was never as bad as that, but could be described as a well-built woman with the most wonderful teeth like pearls — she had only two stoppings in them when aged 70. She had a beautiful, gentle, loving smile as she bent to kiss me goodnight in my bed. She was quite tall — 5'10" — and very fit, with a low resonant speaking voice and a good sense of humour.

When any of us, or indeed our dogs, were ill, she was a most efficient nurse. If the dogs wounded themselves she

25

would stitch them up with cat gut which she cut off the fishing lines! Cotton wool soaked in ether was held a certain distance from the dog's nose to anaesthetize them, and after all her equipment was disinfected she would start stitching. And a very good job she made of it, I can say from experience, as my dog was a whippet who was always tearing herself on wire or staking herself on sticks. Mother never forgot her love of nursing.

As in every big house there was cold war rumbling on between the rest of the staff and Nanny. Open war was not declared till governesses arrived in the years ahead. As Nanny was always on the winning side, such grown-up affairs did not concern me.

The routine in the house was strict and the nursery was no exception. Breakfast at eight, time to play a little, and then a ride with Southgate, the groom who looked after the children's ponies, which was shortened in summer because routine dictated that bathing started about May 15th and stopped on September 30th — the weather had nothing to do with it! Then back to the nursery and to bed for a rest before lunch.

Strangely, I was never taught to swim properly. Father had the idea that you would dog paddle and float and survive if, when very young, you had a cord tied round under your chest and were let over the side of a rowing boat. He was right, we did, but I envy the children who are well instructed today.

The best thing about the bathe was the hard rub down Nanny gave me afterwards and a drink of hot milk from a thermos, with delicious digestive biscuits. Somehow they taste different now to what they did to a cold little girl in the bathing box at Brodick all those years ago.

Little woman that she was, Nanny pushed me up the hill to

The drawing room at Brodick Castle

the castle in the pram from the beach when I was a toddler as indeed she had done to my brothers and sister. The old pram we later called *Wells Fargo* was itself no lightweight, large enough to take a child at both ends, leather-lined, and with a fringed green silk canopy. The climb to the castle from the shore is all of 200 feet and quite steep, though it levels out for a short way along the bottom of the terrace past a great expanse of brilliant azaleas with their glorious smell in Springtime and their wonderful autumn colours later in the year.

From Brodick Bay, one is transfixed by the beauty of the outline of the high peaks of Arran whether in their fierce

The dining room at Brodick Castle

winter mood, or their gentle misty Spring shyness, or their boisterous lively summer holiday mood with yachts sailing round their feet and seagulls gliding beside the boat crowded with tourists. The eye is attracted to the castle which stands proudly at the top of two grass terraces on the north side of Brodick Bay. It stands cosily embraced by woods and fine old trees where the spectacular rocky mass of Goatfell slopes down through heather to the woods finally to kiss the sea below the castle.

Returning from the shore, when Nanny and I arrived at the glass panelled front door we could see the chandelier which hung in the hall from an immense chain descending from the ceiling 80 feet above the hall. When the Spring cleaning took place the estate carpenters climbed into the attic and slowly unwound the chain until the chandelier was low enough for the maids to clean.

Under the stairs stood a large, very old, oak table, the top of which is supposed to be King Robert the Bruce's dining table, though some centuries ago it had new legs fitted.

The climb from the hall to the nursery is up 60 stairs. On the first landing we passed four marble statues of my grandparents and great-grandparents. On the wall hung a life-sized portrait by Maddox of Susan Euphemia, daughter of William Beckford, wife of the 10th Duke, and a portrait of the Duke himself. Between them is a beautiful portrait of my grandfather, the 12th Duke as a little boy in a kilt, with a deer hound, painted by Richard Buckner. From the hall to the nursery floor the whole of one wall is lined with about 100 stags' heads.

The suite of rooms where Mother and Father lived were on the first landing. In these rooms were very fine pictures, pieces of furniture and silver gilt wall sconces by Paul Storr, not that a little girl was interested in such things. What interested me more was that outside every door were black curly mats, to exclude the draught. At that time Mother had black curly cocker spaniels which I fell over more times than I can remember, when I ran along the passage to see her, as they always lay on one or other of the mats.

She liked me to call in and say how I'd got on riding, or what I had done when out with Nanny. Often she would have her secretary there to whom she was dictating letters for she was on an immense number of committees in Arran and on the mainland.

The long picture gallery led from Mother's boudoir to the drawing room. These rooms were part of the house built by

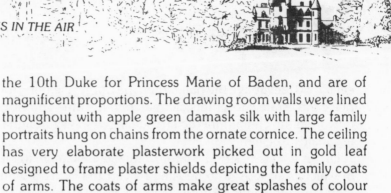

the 10th Duke for Princess Marie of Baden, and are of magnificent proportions. The drawing room walls were lined throughout with apple green damask silk with large family portraits hung on chains from the ornate cornice. The ceiling has very elaborate plasterwork picked out in gold leaf designed to frame plaster shields depicting the family coats of arms. The coats of arms make great splashes of colour right across the ceiling. For big parties the double doors were opened leading into the library, an older part of the castle, the wooden floor of which was laid for dancing. The library led to the dining room and the old walls of Cromwellian days between the library and the dining room are all of eight feet thick and oak panelled.

From the dining room, to get to Robert the Bruce's old part of the castle you have to go down the circular back stairs built into the thickness of the wall of the old tower. The little windows, no more than 2 feet square, are set into the recesses nearly four feet thick. At the foot of the stairs and just below Bruce's room a short distance along the stone back passage lies a sinister story of long ago.

When my mother was repairing and renovating the back quarters she thought she would open the wall which sounded hollow if you tapped it, and see what lay behind, as a secret passage was purported to lead from the shore to this point. A heap of rubble fell out. By luck, she took me to visit Willie Davidson who farmed Glen Rosa and whose family had been there as long as my family had been in Brodick. He told her that three women had contracted the plague in 1700 and their bodies had been thrown down a disused secret passage leading to the shore, and quicklime and rubble had been tipped on top of them. When we got home my mother instructed the builders to replace the rubble and plaster up the hole and make no further excavations in case any germs would escape!

I don't think Nanny had any family so she seldom took a holiday or had a day off. During the only two long holidays I remember Nanny having she spent the entire time with the Lloyds with whom she had worked before coming to us — the only other family she had worked for, in fact.

What paragons of virtue those Lloyds were! Jack and Buba Lloyd, it appeared, had never put a foot wrong in all their childhood days, whereas I never seemed to put one right. The two holidays were traumatic as far as I was concerned.

Once I remember her going out in the evening when my mother sent her by car to the neighbouring village of Sannox for dinner with friends. I stayed awake for her return and, sleepy though I was, I became aware that through the open door leading to the day nursery grown-ups were talking, and I sensed there was a worry because Nanny was so late coming back. Surely there could not have been an accident? Could they have run out of petrol? And so the chatter went on. I lay very quiet and listened, very frightened something had happened. Then, joy of joys, I heard the old familiar voice arrive back in the nursery. I leapt up and ran through to join the grown-ups.

"Lawks alive, can't I go out without you playing up?"

"Nanny, what happened, what happened?" as tears rolled down my cheeks.

"Now wait till I get my teeth out and I'll tell you."

When Nanny's gnashers were safe behind the photograph frame she told how two stags had got onto the lawn of the house where she was having supper and started fighting right by the front door. They got their antlers entangled and had fought on till in the end one was killed.

I was so terrified to hear this story, late at night, that the size

31

Display of deer antlers on the wall of the staircase of Brodick Castle

of the stags became the size of elephants in my imagination and for nights I would not go to sleep till I could curl up with Nanny in her bed. The lights had to be left on till she was there.

The hall and staircase at Brodick Castle are lined from the ground floor to the ceiling with stags' heads, stuffed and with great brown glass eyes stuck in them reflecting the light. Nobody knew the fear those heads caused us children when we were sent down after tea to play in the drawing room with Mother and Father. Nanny usually took us down, but getting back to the nursery on our own was the trouble. I don't think Mother ever related the fact that I had heard the story of the fight and associated these heads staring down at me with the fighting stags, now grown out of all proportion. For a time I refused to go up alone, but the day came when I had to, and shame on me, I nearly wet my pants as I ran so hard with fair hair flying out behind me and red shoes and white socks flashing up the stairs as fast as I could go — and what a long way it was to a little girl.

Being kid sister I had to refer to friends of the family as "Mr" or "Miss". Unfortunately Nanny had a little trouble with her aitches and one day I referred to Alan Ebber Percy. The grown-ups guffawed with laughter but did not tell me why, so I tried again,

"Mr. Ebber Percy ......" — more laughter, so he just became "that man" and it was not till I was reading through the visitors' book that I found out that Mr. Alan Hebber Percy had been to stay.

Mother was caught out once when she asked how my new dress had been torn.

"On the edge," Nanny said.

"The edge of what?" Mother asked. "The edge of the steps, or what?"

"No," said Nanny, "that dark green 'edge with the yellow flowers, growing from the back door to the drive."!

Being so very much younger than the rest of the family I knew the other children very little, as they were at boarding school. I got a severe ticking off from Nanny when she heard me shouting from the top of the stairs,

"Boy! Boy! Come and play with me!"

"How dare you call him 'boy'! Don't you know that is your brother Ronald?"

3

TRIBULATIONS OF AN ENGLISH NANNY

NE morning when I was about three, returning from the beach I complained that my foot hurt when I jumped off a bank. I must have complained often because Mother asked me to jump again and show her where it hurt. She found a swelling.

It was the start of tuberculous osteitis. It was ironic because Mother was a keen and knowledgeable farmer and had one of the first farms in Arran, (in fact in the County of Bute,) to be tested and cleared of T.B. I suppose her herd must have been low in butterfat because she bought a Jersey cow and took it for granted that the Farm Manager would isolate it and have it tested before putting it in the herd. This was not done, and the rich Jersey milk was sent up to the nursery. That was the start of many frustrations and difficulties later in my life. There were no antibiotics in those days and the cure was rest and sun (or carbon arc lights giving ultra violet rays) and calcium pills and cod liver oil.

It was not long after my sore foot was discovered that Mother took Nanny and me to Professor Rollier's Sanatorium for tuberculosis at Leysin, in Switzerland, as his work on the disease was becoming well known. An abscess was cut out of my ankle and my leg was put in irons for many months. Nanny and I were left out there and, in fact, stayed for a year.

Poor Nanny. It was every English nanny's nightmare to be left surrounded by a lot of foreigners who could not even make a good cup of tea. Besides, she belonged to the old school when the staff had a beer ration every day. Nanny, who did not like beer, had a ration of Guinness's Sweet Stout

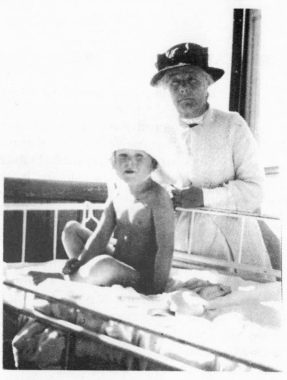

Nanny and me, aged three, in the Clinic at Leysin

which she kept in the boot cupboard off the night nursery at home, and, of course, Messrs. Guinness had not penetrated Professor Rollier's clinic. To make matters worse she slipped and broke her leg and lay in the next bed to me with a big arch, with blue lights, covering the injury. That was one-up-manship, and I coveted that bit of equipment all my stay there.

The big event of the day was throwing breadcrumbs to the black birds with scarlet bills and legs. Nanny called them

Schukas (they were, in fact, choughs). They fluttered down onto the balcony disturbing the newly fallen snow by their dozens and it passed many a long hour for me.

My bed was wheeled out into the sun for a regulated length of time for me to sunbathe, then wheeled back indoors. Sometimes, when outside, I was given a white clay pipe and a cup of soapy water and taught to blow soap bubbles which drifted away in the sun. It must have been difficult for the grown-ups to occupy a child of three in bed for nearly nine months.

Eventually I was allowed up and out into the garden with a G-string on and nothing else, which enabled a bumble bee to sting me where no-one should be stung!

Mother and Father came to visit me once or twice and then the whole family came out over the Christmas holidays and leased a chalet. It was a big event to have my family round me again, but I saw little of them. They went skiing and skated, in which I could not join them.

When Spring came and the family had gone home, Nanny hired a pony sledge and we drove down to the valley to the snow line. The driver unharnessed the horse and hobbled it, leaving Nanny and me wandering among the wonderful Spring flowers. He went off and cut twigs of willow or birch and wove them together like a large bird's nest with a handle, then filled the nest with bright green moss and arranged flowers of every kind and colour in the moss. These nests were the prettiest gift you can imagine and one of the happier memories I have of Leysin.

The great day came when I got home to all that was familiar to me, and Nanny had a proper cup of tea once again.

Before I went to Switzerland I had already been initiated to the art of riding. From about two years onwards I was dressed

up and put into a chair-like saddle on the pony's back. It was a soft padded white kid leather chair with a belt across my tummy to stop me falling out. On fine afternoons I rode around the garden paths led by Mr. Southgate. He looked after the childrens' ponies and the governess cart, a smart brown varnished trap which was entered from the rear and had a highly polished brass rail round the front. There was also a tiny trap pulled by Paddy the goat, but he proved to be of too uncertain temper and bolted when a friend was in it. I must confess I gave him a biff on the backside and he and Susan Ridley, a godchild of my mother's, disappeared down the drive where she was flung out into the rhododendron bushes. That was the end of Paddy.

When I returned from Switzerland I was promoted to a proper saddle and was sent out riding in the morning. Nanny

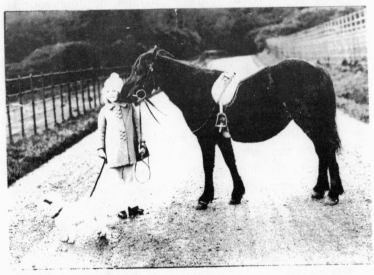

Myself and Companions

and I would go out with Southgate in the governess trap in the afternoon. Southgate was London-born and started to work for my family in the Easton stables. He was a dapper little man with an india-rubbery face inclined to smile. On hot summer days he wore a straw boater, otherwise a cloth cap when leading ponies, and a bowler when riding. At all times he wore a white butterfly collar, riding breeches and black leather leggings, highly polished.

Most afternoons Southgate came up to the front door of the Castle with Victory, the bay mare born on Victory Day 1918, who pulled the trap, to await Nanny and me. The wait depended on what there had been for lunch because children in those days were not allowed fads and fancies, nor were we allowed to waste food. We were told to "think of the starving Russians" who were the people at that moment in history who apparently would have absolutely loved my tapioca pudding looking like frog's eyes and just as slimy. They also were crazy about bloody roast beef — I am not swearing — I mean beef that was bloody, oozing blood onto my plate. Unfortunately there were no obliging Russians near and Victory had to stand champing her bit at the door for as long as the tapioca was going round and round in my mouth.

On the days of boiled chicken and spinach followed by any fattening pudding, I reached the door at the same time as Victory and at the flick of the whip we would clip clop our way up the shore road to the next village of Corrie, five miles to the north. I enjoyed the fresh sea breeze blowing up the brim of my hat, tightening the elastic band under my chin. I watched the sea birds on the rocks and the acres of yellow flags, the wild iris, blowing against the background of the blue sea. The smell of the yellow gorse was heavy in the air. Sometimes we stopped and watched a seal on the red sandstone rocks or watched the menacing black triangular fin of a basking shark gliding along the shore parallel to us.

We arrived in time to see the cruising steamer slow down about a hundred yards off the rocky Corrie shore at Ferry Rock, and the summer tourists being rowed out to her in three big ferry boats. Up the gangway went the outgoing tourists then the newcomers disembarked, a difficult operation on a windy day. We could hear, quite distinctly, the band playing on deck, a concertina, a violin and goodness knows what else. They played the songs of the day or good rousing old Scottish airs and the passengers would join in and sing. We would turn Victory round and if we could persuade her to show any speed, keep pace with the boat for quite a long way. After that we relied on Southgate's large repertoire of stories and songs which included one which started "Little Willie had a monkey on a yellow stick" and went on and on till poor little Willie died because he had licked the stick and swallowed the yellow paint.

"There you are, you see," Nanny could be guaranteed to say. "Remember what I've told you about putting things in your mouth."

In fact, we were allowed to put nothing in our mouths when we were out, not even ice cream, which I thought was unfair, but now I see the sense because if you go on any journey anywhere today a great part of the Scottish public never stop from the beginning to the end of the journey pushing something into their mouths. I often feel like asking if they have never heard of Little Willie.

Nanny sat like a Queen on her side of the trap, bolt upright, eyes well shaded by her large hat and when Southgate was not singing ditties to me they would have one of those maddening grown-up conversations.

"You know who, well the other day they said they saw that

couple you know what."

"Who are you talking about Nanny? Who is it? What did they do? Nanny, but what *DID* they do?"

"Oh be quiet, child. Listeners hear no good of themselves. Look at those deer up there," she would say, with a sweep of her arm.

"Where, Nanny? Where are they?" — I knew I had been duped and by the time I had looked for the deer I never knew who the couple was or what had been seen or said.

As I looked back along the road to the receding line of whitewashed cottages at Corrie with their whitewashed garden walls I could see several herring smacks sailing to their fishing grounds, their red-brown sails bending as they caught the wind. Corrie boasted quite a little fleet in those days as did several other Arran villages before the days of the highly sophisticated, very costly, motor ships.

Looking from the Corrie shore I could see a lot of small craft plying their coastal trade along the shores of the islands of Bute and Cumbrae and down the coast of Ayrshire. All coal and farm manures were brought over to Arran in sailing skiffs which landed their cargoes on various flat beaches round the island. Then there was a veritable fleet of Para Handy's *Vital Spark* boats. Painted with red hulls and black and white superstructures, chugging along with black smoke issuing from their funnels. Corrie harbour was a regular port of call where they unloaded goods and collected red cut sandstone that the estate sold and from which a lot of houses in Glasgow were built.

It was always the sea I watched and the sea I remember. The hills were there but to me they were the backdrop, dead except when the stags were roaring. I took in their beauty, the beauty of the old whitewashed cottages of the clachan of High Corrie high up above the village, now the home of one

of Scotland's most famous writers, Robert McLellan, nestling at the foot of Am Bennan. I saw the white gash of foaming water flowing over the solid slabs of granite rocks well named the White Water. I saw, but to a child it was the outside world, and my cosy secure world was the little pony trap with Southgate and his songs, and Nanny, and we were going home to tea.

4

STAFF HIERARCHY OF TWO CASTLES

 HE hierarchy inside the castles was no less strict than outside. Both Brodick and Buchanan had its butler and housekeeper who did not travel backwards and forwards between the two places. The difference was one of character, not of position. Georgie Prentice, housekeeper at Brodick, was a little cottage loaf of a woman whose shining face was full of twinkle though she had a temper when she wanted. The housekeeper at Buchanan was an impressive dark woman with dark eyes and a hairy face. I called her 'Old Snib the Windy' because during my first winter at Buchanan I heard a shindy beyond the door at the end of the nursery passage where she was ranting and raging at some feckless girl newly arrived to learn her trade.

"You didna' snib the windies as you ought! It's nae good standing there arguing with me for ye ken fine you didna' snib the windies as you ought!"

At Brodick Mr.Allan, the butler, was a distinguished presence to be reckoned with. I cannot remember much about Mr. Lay at Buchanan. In both places the housekeeper was responsible for all the female staff other than in the nursery and kitchen. The ladies maid and the valet were their own masters, directly under the orders of my parents. Nanny was certainly her own master and master of most other people, also she had a nursery maid when the other three children were babies. The poor governess was indeed on her own and master of none.

Back in history the distilling of beers and various medicines took place in the stillroom but latterly, under the jurisdiction

43

Buchanan Castle

of the housekeeper, the stillroom maids did all the decorating of cakes and made all the pastries, jams and chutneys, marmalades and pickles. When the castle was full we used three to four pounds of jam each day, plus honey and marmalade, not allowing for any which might be used in cooking.

Georgie Prentice was in charge of the four housemaids for the cleaning of the house, mending and issuing of the linen and the store cupboards of cleaning materials. My mother gave her orders to Georgie as to which rooms were to be used for guests, and she saw that the rooms were ready for their arrival. In conjunction with the Clerk of Works she would get the carpenters to repair any furniture or windows or doors. Every carpet was lifted for Spring cleaning and

44

beaten with cane bats (long canes with plaited woven ends the shape of a bat).

Georgie Prentice had started with my family when she was 14 years of age as stillroom maid and only left for a short time to work for the Duke of Buckingham at Stowe before she returned to us. She had left us because the staff when off duty were supposed to wear a uniform and rightly she objected to that.

Mr.Henry Allan, the butler, had also been with the family since he was 14 years old when he started to work for my Grandmother, the Duchess of Hamilton. Before his retirement he had served four generations of my family. He was six foot tall, with a lugubrious face and bushy eyebrows, and he was a very distinguished looking gentleman. We children were all afraid of him. My chief memory is that when I and my friends, on a lovely hot summer evening, had been playing tennis, and perhaps we had been tempted to finish the game regardless of the fact that we should have been dressing for dinner, or maybe we had been out in the boat fishing for mackerel and when there's a good take of mackerel and we pulled in the lines as hard as we could with two or three fish on a line at one time, dressing for dinner seems a remote discipline and time slips by. When we realised how late it was we would rush in through the back door and up the corkscrew wooden stairs, but on reaching the point half way up where the staircase branched to the left going to the butler's pantry and the dining room, a large figure dressed in pin-striped trousers and a cutaway coat and a large gold watch chain would be standing, leaning against the wall. He would give us a severe dressing down.

"Do you suppose I am going to keep my men late on duty just because you young scalliwags can't get in on time? Have you no thought for other people? What do you suppose I am

45

Mr Henry Allan with the four generations he served. From left to right: Mrs Sellar and her daughter Isobel, Marchioness of Graham; Lady Fiona Graham; Lady Mary Boscawen and her son James; the Duchess of Montrose; the Duchess of Hamilton

to say to Her Grace if dinner's late?"

"Oh, please, Mr. Allan, please just keep dinner back for five minutes, we'll never do this again, we'll be so quick!" and we would scamper up the stairs.

I can't say we had a bath — we merely slid through the water and flung on the clothes that had been laid out for us on the bed by the maid. I would shout to my friends to make sure that we all went down at the same time — I was less likely to get a ticking off from Mother that way! We would run downstairs along the corridor to the drawing room door and put the brakes on just in time to open the door and make a dignified entrance. My mother would say:

"You're late — very lucky for you the cook seems to be late, too. I hope this won't happen again."

46

We would just have time to apologise when the double doors leading through the library into the dining room would open and Mr. Allan, with a totally expressionless face, would announce,

"Dinner is served, Your Grace."

It's very late," my mother would say.

"An unavoidable delay," he would say with great dignity, and then make his sedate way into the dining room waiting for my mother and the guests, and never by look or word did he give us away. I think he must have been standing behind the library door listening for us to enter the drawing room before announcing the meal.

It was just a year or two before the Second World War that "Progress" struck him very hard when my mother announced that she was not employing another footman but in future would be employing parlourmaids. She tried to assure him that other big houses in Britain were now employing parlourmaids. I don't think he ever believed her and he felt he had come down considerably in lifestyle. However, we were lucky insofar that the first parlourmaid, Chrissie, was extremely good at her work and very nice, and when the second parlourmaid came she was equally good. I stopped in my tracks one evening when passing the pantry door, having heard singing, and through the door I saw Henry Allan and the two parlourmaids dancing the Palais Glide! Progress seemed to have some advantages!

It was always a slight worry to my parents that they did not give Mr. Allan and Mrs. Prentice their places by calling them by their surnames. Instead, they were always called "Georgie" and "Henry" because the old habits are not easy to break.

Many years later when they had both retired and Mr. Allan was widowed, after working together for fifty years they married and lived in a cottage in Brodick until they died. He felt he had to make some justification to my mother and he told her that it seemed easier to divide the work in the way they had always done in the past, and it was easier to do that in the same house!

In the days when living was hard, it was a great thing for the local cottagers if they could get one child placed in the castle, probably aged about 14 years, where he or she would be well looked after and have the most thorough education on how to look after a house. They were fed very well though it was not unusual for the agreement of employment to read that "salmon, venison, mackerel and rabbit should not be served to them more than once a week". At the age of 14 they were never seen or expected to be seen in the front of the house. The girls acted as maids to the housekeeper or the head housemaid and the young kitchen maid acted as ladies maid to the cook. It was their job in the morning to call these esteemed ladies with a tray of morning tea, to draw their curtains, and shut their windows, and light their bedroom fires. The girl then had to lay out the head housemaid's brushes, dusters and dustpan on the window sill on the back stairs near her bedroom and do her personal laundry, and the kitchen maid had to go down and start preparing the servants' breakfasts. Having done this it was their job to call the guests and myself and the ladies maid's job to call my mother, and the valet's job to call my father with a tray of morning tea and usually a small plate of the most delicious fine, fine cut bread and butter. Oh, it was so good.

The same applied to male staff, the boot boy or hall boy had to call the butler in the same way, and then go and lay the servants' breakfast, both in the Stewards' Room where the head people ate and in the Servants' Hall, carry the trays and have the meals laid.

It was only after a considerable time that these young

things were considered sufficiently trained to proceed up the ladder of promotion either in the house where they had been trained or they could apply for a reference and then try to get a job in another house of similar standing. However, should they have proved unsatisfactory and were unable to get a reference, their future was gloomy indeed, and they would never get a job in a big house again.

The footmen, of which there were three, wore black trousers and a dark bottle green cutaway coat, brass buttons with the family crest on them, and starched waistcoats of green and yellow stripes. This was the Montrose livery, the Hamilton livery was a black and scarlet waistcoat.

As butler, Mr. Allan was in charge of three footmen and had the responsibility of seeing all the silver in the house was clean. He would turn in his grave if he knew what had happened to me.

When my mother died, the Trustees said I could take three really good silver ornaments, as the rest had to be handed to the Treasury in lieu of death duties. I chose three Ausberg silver gilt animals, which I kept locked up nearly all the time. However, one summer when I had rather a smart shooting party I had the ornaments on the dining room table and I noticed one evening that the silver was showing through the gilt. I meant to draw this to the attention of the temporary women working for me but forgot the next morning. Next day more silver showed, so I questioned them at once as to what they were using to clean them.

"Brasso."

"For heaven's sakes, why?"

"Well, they are brass, aren't they?"

"Would I be likely to put brass on the table just when I had guests? They are silver gilt!"

"Well, they should be in a museum, then."

49

What an answer. Just because someone is too lazy to ask what to do. No apology, nothing, yet by foolishness hundreds of pounds were lost and now the ornaments have to be locked up in the castle safe. I could tell many stories like that to illustrate the great knowledge these people in the old days acquired in handling antiques. It was a big responsibility for them.

The silver which was in daily use was cleaned or rubbed up with great frequency but that which was in the safe was cleaned in rotation, one shelf per day. The layout of silver in the dining room was changed daily as there was little not in use.

There was a strict demarcation line between the men's work and the housemaid's work, so if a footman should be seen to rub a cloth over a table top it insulted the housemaid and if the maid rubbed up a silver ashtray or inkpot it insulted the footman! There were frequent battles.

It may seem strange today to people looking back at the high esteem in which these head servants were held, but they really did have great responsibility.

Mr. Allan had the responsibility of shutting up the house at night which was always an insoluble problem. If any staff were out for the evening he had to wait up for their return. Having to return early from a party was a great point of complaint with the maids and I myself thought arrangements could have been made for each to have a key. I tried it when I had a house of my own and found I could not rely on the girls taking their key with them, so half the time they got locked out by me when I went to bed and as often as not they lost their keys. I had to replace the locks three times in one summer. Obviously a man who had done a hard day's work could not sit up night after night to let the girls in, so there seemed to be no satisfactory way to resolve the complaint.

The male staff had their rooms in a separate wing across the back yard so they could come and go as they pleased.

A long way down the ladder was "the odd man". His title depicts his work — everything that was no-one else's job, plucking birds, scrubbing the stone back passages, carrying logs and coal all the way up to the bedrooms. What a weight it must have been! He brought up the nursery and schoolroom meals and stoked the boiler and the kitchen range which burned one hundredweight of coal a day at Brodick. They seemed to be ex-servicemen as a rule, and George Hay who died in 1979 had some fine stories to tell. He was a great friend of Nanny's for years, being one of the gambling set; but the friendship cooled after a day when he was on his way to Cladoch to pick up the Castle private mail bag and an aeroplane flew over his head, which was an uncommon event then. From the telephone call box in Cladoch he phoned and placed his bet on "Aeroplane", an outsider, and did not tell Nanny. He won a lot of money.

Bobby the valet, son of the head keeper at Dougarie, eventually took over from Mr. Allan as butler. He was quite a different character, fairly small in stature with a bit of a lisp and he talked very fast, getting his words muddled — "Here's your grouses, Grace, your Grouse" — as an instance!

The kitchen and the cook remained a mystery because it was the same in all big houses, that the young were not allowed in, so all I remember of the cooks who came and went is a raised arm with the forefinger pointing to the door and a screamed "GET OUT"!

Now I am the cook in my own house I quite understand why they were all bad tempered! The only occasions when I went into the kitchen was when in the Spring nettles were collected to make soup and spinach, and also young dandelions.

At Buchanan, long before farmers used poisons and

dressed corn seed, the woods by the river Endrick were plagued with rooks. In the evening the sky was darkened by thousands of the birds coming to roost. We used to shoot the young ones newly out of the nest in Spring and I took these birds to the kitchen where the most delicious hot or cold pies, succulent with herbs, were made. Father announced with great regularity that the very thought of eating rooks made him sick, just as he was finishing his second helping of a pie he believed to be pigeon! He maintained he could not eat rabbit. One Sunday when my grandmother was a guest for lunch she saw he had half a wishbone on his plate.

"I see you can now eat rabbit," she said.

"No I cannot. You know very well it makes me sick."

"Well, that is a rib bone and the lump on the end is where it joins the spine, 'ain't it?" (that generation used 'ain't' quite usually).

Mother started to laugh because for once the casserole was of chicken which at that time was considered a luxury dish.

"Molly, you have not given me rabbit, have you? You know it makes me sick." But before she could answer he put his napkin over his mouth and made a hasty retreat!

The cook controlled the assistant cooks and a scullery maid. For no reason I can give, the scullery maid had to wash up the dining room meat plates. On one occasion at Brodick the plate rack above her sink came away from the wall and the whole set of 70 plates were broken. She was not hurt, luckily, but greatly shocked.

One of the last cooks Mother had at Brodick, poor old soul, had lost her memory. There was a long wait for the savoury — Father did not like rich puddings — and eventually the butler came to the dining room to announce that Cook had lost the savoury. We all rose from table and a sort of "hunt the savoury" took place. We eventually found it on top of the cupboard pushed well to the back! The same old girl, when making a boiled rice pudding, forgot to put the rice into the milk!

CASTLES IN THE AIR

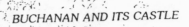

5

BUCHANAN AND ITS CASTLE

**Y paternal** grandfather, the 5th Duke of Montrose, was a big man with a moustache who called me 'Curly Tops' and ran his fingers through my silver fair hair. I only remember seeing him twice before he died in November 1925.

His mother, Caroline, wife of the 4th Duke of Montrose, was known as "The Racing Duchess". During her life the old Buchanan House was burnt down because she was away from home so much she did not know that her housekeeper drank. She raced under the name of "Mr. Manton", as women could not register horses at the Jockey Club in those days. She won the Derby in 1880 with her horse *Sefton*. Her jockey was the famous Fred Archer, and their friendship caused many raised eyebrows.

Granny Montrose was very earnest, tall, thin and extremely beautiful and ran a sort of keep fit class for her family. They had to have cold baths in the morning and then skip with a skipping rope half-way down the drive of Buchanan Castle. She herself kept this up till she was in her late seventies. Their food was very simple and they all had a fear of rich food or drink all their days. She had never been a country woman like my Hamilton Grandmother and Mother, so living in a city, as she did when widowed, did not worry or confine her. So uncountryfied was she that one day, at the farm where she accompanied my grandfather when he had gone to see his prize bull, she was overheard to say,

"Really, Ronald, why must you keep such a dangerous animal when all I want is a little milk for the house?"!

Sir George Leith Buchanan, Mother, Granny Montrose,
the Rev. Goldie, Lady Helen Graham.
Lady Helen was Lady-in-Waiting to the Queen Mother from when the
Queen married till my Aunt died in 1945

Grandpapa was mainly interested in steeplechasing and had fences made in the park which was his training ground, now famed as Buchanan Golf Course.

The stable block at Buchanan, near the ruin of the old house, had been built in the days of the 3rd Duke of Montrose who was Master of the King's Horse. That position he held from 1783 until 1789, and as one of the perquisites he had permission to use the Bay Team of the King's Horses to pull his carriage when he travelled. There being no suitable stables at Buchanan to house such a distinguished team of horses, new and suitable horse boxes and stalls were

built in the shape of a huge square with a cobbled yard in the centre, with an ornamental pump and drinking trough in the middle. Round the yard were the stables. When the race-horses were stabled there the sides of the boxes were padded with straw held in place by hessian sacking so the horses could not knock and damage themselves.

The Buchanan estate stretched from Kilmaronock up the east bank of Loch Lomond to Inversnaid, east to the centre of Loch Katrine, Loch Achray, and Gartmore including Chapplearoch.

When my Montrose grandfather died in 1925 we spent Christmas at Brodick that year so that renovations to Buchanan Castle could be carried out. There was only one bathroom in the entire 40 roomed castle! Hot water had to be carried from the kitchen on the ground floor to the nursery, two floors up, and at the other end of the castle. I remember the fascination of bathing in a hip bath in front of the big fire in the day nursery. Huge brass cans of hot water were poured into the brown tin bath, painted white inside. Mother put in 13 bathrooms!

After the fire of 1852 the new Buchanan Castle was built on top of a hill looking south over a beautiful wide expanse of parkland which was my grandfather's racehorse training course, with magnificent trees standing in groups showing their full beauty and shape. Looking west over wooded land was Loch Lomond and the hills beyond.

As well as having 40 bedrooms, the castle had a gallery where 200—300 couples could dance, with an orchestra sitting in a bay with bow windows of coloured glass which had the coats of arms of the family depicted on them. Twenty-seven servants were employed and it was the scene of many great parties in my father's youth. Many illustrious guests were invited, amongst whom were the Comte de

View along the terrace at Buchanan

The Gallery at Buchanan, where we could dance two hundred couples

Paris, King Victor Emmanuel of Italy and the Shah of Persia — who fascinated the family by blowing his nose on the curtains!

In the dining room there were three windows reaching from the floor to the cornice, and on one side hung Van Dyke's famous portrait of King Charles on a white charger which latterly my father gave to Her Majesty the Queen to hang in Holyrood Palace. At the other end of the dining room was a full length portrait of William Pitt, and the fourth wall was occupied by a magnificent Jasper fireplace, carved from the marble vein running beside Loch Lomond.

The castle was crowned by turrets so popular in Victorian days, and on the highest turret above the front door stood "The Watchman", a life-sized figure of a Highlander blowing a trumpet and holding a pike in his hand. The castle was surrounded by an Arboratum of specimen fir trees backed by acres of forest. The three drives leading to the castle were each well over a mile in length.

In my childhood, the days of living in a castle with 40 bedrooms were over and gone, except for high days and holidays, so actually we lived in one wing of the castle. I am afraid Buchanan depressed me very much, but Father, of course, loved his old home and remembered it as it was when in full swing. My depression was partly because we lived there during the wet, grey Scottish winters, and also because the house was grey and, when driving up the front drive, the first view to greet one was the front door, locked and bolted. We had to turn right onto a small drive and round the building to the door we used. This door was on the north side of the building and got no sun, so the lawn by the door was mostly moss — the dark green, wet kind of moss.

Of much more concern was a deep, artificially made pool with wooden planks round the side, situated in the wood 300 yards to the north. In fact, it was a water supply in case of fire. To prevent me going near it at any time Nanny told me there was an octopus (which she pronounced Ock-Topaze) in it, which had eight vast legs which it could swing over the side and snatch little girls if they went anywhere near. I need hardly say I kept well clear, and even when I knew there was no monster living there it still held a dread for me.

Our wing was quite self-contained. The entrance door led directly on to a circular staircase of grey stone. The first landing was where my Mother and Father lived, and up a lot more stairs the day and night nurseries, the schoolroom, and governess's room were situated. The top floor consisted of a sitting room and the bedrooms of my sister and my two brothers. The covering of the passages was simplicity itself, the nursery floor was covered with coia matting and there was lino on the top floor. It makes one wonder where the myth of the plush living of the aristocracy comes from, for sure it had nothing to do with central heating in old Scottish castles or our life at Buchanan! You could have sailed a boat with your umbrella up in most of the corridors!

We were all tomboys and ragged a great deal, and had some real rough and tumbles. I was too young to join in with the others and their friends who played passage football till the house shook. My playmate was my cousin Margaret Graham, daughter of my Uncle Alastair, and our game was sliding down the flights of polished oak stairs in the front portion of the castle until the seats of our pants came out. I don't know why we did not break our backs, we went so fast.

Once we had got ourselves settled in at Buchanan the rhythm of family life was that from November 1st or thereabouts till the end of April we were at Buchanan and then moved to Brodick and Dougarie for the summer.

In my day the racehorses had long gone and my ponies

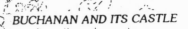

occupied the boxes. Now, when I go into some smart restaurant where the vogue is to cover the walls with hessian, I think of the stable at Buchanan and have visions of my rough and shaggy little Welsh pony, Peter, with his mane and forelock standing every which way in his palatial loose box with all the cheek in the world. Did he realize he occupied the box of some departed thoroughbred?

By the age of six I was somewhat more proficient at riding. Peter was a perfect child's pony and very good natured. I

Myself on Roany, in 1928

used to lead him up the steps, into the back passage and along to the kitchen where he was given bits of carrot or sugar. Each day I had to ride on a different saddle. One day the side saddle would have the pummels on the right of the pony, and one day on the left, and the third day I rode astride. This routine was to keep my hips straight because my mother

had one hip nearly two inches higher than the other which was thought to be due to having ridden so much on one side saddle. It was considered very Non-U to ride sidesaddle with a balance strap, and even when out hunting she only used it with one horse who kicked sideways on top of his jump which would have dislodged the very best rider or loosened the saddle.

I was no horsewoman, and if ever I met my mother or Grandmother when out riding, I was always accused of being like a sack of potatoes, or my hands were too high, or my heels too low. All the ponies and horses I rode seemed to know I did not like them any more than they liked me which led to many disasters.

For the winter Mother's hunters were now stabled near Paisley and rooms were found for the groom to be near them. She hunted two days a week because horse boxes as we know them today had not come into fashion by then.

Paisley was well situated for hunting with the Lanark and Renfrew pack. She was driven to the meet by Tommy Watson in the Studebaker, leaving Buchanan at about 8.30 a.m., with its perspex windows flapping in the cold winter winds. She sat in the back with her bowler hat and veil and a smart white stock kept in place with two gold tie pins, thick riding jacket and habit with breeches to match, and black leather boots polished till you could see your face in them. The groom got to the meet before her with three horses. She loved her days out, always had good horses, and went well across country. Even the rough Scottish days did not put her off her sport though she looked back in fondness to her days down South.

When I was older a horse was hired for me from the Youngs' Livery Stable at Paisley and I would accompany her on a Saturday. Looking back, I wonder why I did not have the courage to say I did not enjoy those muddy cold, wet, grey days, and was frozen stiff and scared to death. One did not argue with grown-ups in those days, and if one was taken hunting, then hunting one went.

The Master of Hounds, Mr. Collins, had a daughter, Pat, of my age and there were lots of young people whom I enjoyed meeting. Sometimes I was allowed to stay with Pat Collins at their home *Barrochan* and was collected by Mother after the next hunting day.

My life at Buchanan was much the same as at Brodick, governess and schoolroom in the term time, and Nanny for the holidays. When it was not too frosty I rode each afternoon but when the weather was hard there was splendid skating and tobogganing. Two winters I remember as being very hard indeed and crowds of people came to Loch Lomond to skate. The loch was frozen so hard we could skate out to some of the islands or along the 29 mile length of the loch. There were big competitions for curling (bonspiel) and the whole of Balmaha Bay was crowded with players. Father remembered, when he was a young man and the winters were more severe, taking a horse and cart to Inchcailleach, the island half a mile from Balmaha, with turnips to feed fallow deer which were kept there.

Several days we drove over to Port of Menteith to watch curling matches and Bonspeils. These days were the greatest fun as everyone from ploughman to Duke were out to have a good time. Refreshments, both solid and liquid, flowed and it was like the scenes one sees depicted in many of the pictures by old masters on the rivers and canals of long, long ago. Every winter there was sure to be curling and skating on the Drymen curling pond, which was specially prepared in autumn when the rushes and grass were cut and the curlers' hut painted, and the steps up to the hut were cleared. When

Myself, at the
tuberculosis
clinic at Leysin
in Switzerland

the pond froze Drymen would challenge each of the surrounding villages to a curling match. One end of the pond
was kept for skating. There were plenty of spaces to
toboggan, and even a few short runs where the older ones
could practice skiing.

Christmas each year was a busy time. On Christmas Eve
presents were given to the family and the house staff around
a tree fully twelve feet tall, decorated from top to bottom with
tinsel, crackers, coloured glass balls and — what makes one
gasp now — real lighted candles! They were lit by a taper
tied to the end of a bamboo cane and, while alight, someone
was posted on duty with a wet sponge tied to another
bamboo cane. The only safeguard was one or two Minimax
appliances moved near to the tree in case the worst happened.
If one were to face facts neither the wet sponge or the
Minimax appliance could have controlled a twelve foot
Christmas tree when once ablaze.

We had all the usual Christmas games of dooking for
apples afloat in a bucket of water, with your hands tied
behind your back or snatching raisins from the flames of
lighted brandy, etc., or we played charades or guessing the

smells of various liquids in bottles. On Christmas Day there was a party for the school children. At Brodick it was held in the Hall, at Buchanan it was held in the castle. There was a large number of children in both places, certainly not less than sixty, and Mother spent days choosing and buying presents for each child and schoolmaster and mistress and, with help, packed the toys and wrote the name on each label. A huge tea was provided and crackers, nuts and oranges supplied. In the end it grew too big, and the Womens' Rural Institute took over the parties in both places.

Christmas at Buchanan was much more fun than at Brodick. There was one childrens' party after another in the county and, of course, we had at least one at Buchanan. For this the main corridor and dining room were opened and a conjuror or a film hired.

The day nursery at Buchanan was a long, narrow, rather poky little room. Nanny had an equally narrow little bedroom where, during her fairly frequent bouts of gout, she would sit soaking her feet in a footbath full of very hot water and Epsom Salts and a bath towel over her knees to keep her warm, keening to herself for comfort. My room was next to hers, both near to the schoolroom, a large sunny room looking down over the garden and the trees to Loch Lomond in the distance.

Nanny's crystal set sat on a table by her chair near the fire. It had glowing bulbs at the top and a lot of wires and aerials. She sat with her earphones on and, only occasionally, if I was a very good girl, was I allowed to listen to Childrens' Hour — usually Miss Garscadden who ran the Childrens' Programmes in Glasgow, known as Auntie Kathleen. When the radio went wrong, which was fairly often, Nanny rang the bell to get the footman, Matthew, to come up and mend it for her. He was

supposed to know all about such things.

It seems odd that a religious country like Scotland should completely ignore the main religious festivals such as Christmas, the birth of Christ, or his death at Easter. When I was a child Christmas was a normal working day.

The first Christmas at Buchanan Father took me for a walk down the front drive where we saw the woodmen felling trees and burning up the branches and rubbish on a huge bonfire. Lying at the edge of the road was a man so drunk he was incapable of moving. I thought he was dead and, of course, was very curious and excited about him and asked my father if he was dead. Father said simply that he was drunk and went to instruct the woodmen to carry him close to the warmth of the fire, and explained no more to me.

The following week a very upright, respectable little widow, Mrs. Murray of Purnie Hall, came to call on my mother for tea. Father had gone out for a walk earlier in the afternoon and had not returned, which always gave Mother much concern because his middle ear deafness meant he lost his balance completely in the dark or in fog and was apt to lurch sideways or even fall. Mother was afraid he would lurch in front of a car or fall getting over a fence or ditch. As time went on I could see my mother was getting more and more anxious and conversation with Mrs. Murray more and more stilted, so I thought I would comfort Mother, and said,

"Don't worry, he is probably drunk and lying in the ditch."

Not knowing that the previous week I had seen the drunk woodman, she gave one bound and caught me by the hand or even my pigtail, I cannot remember which, and then pushed me out of the sitting room; she was furious with me. I have a vague impression of the *pince nez* jumping off Mrs. Murray's nose in utter shock. I burst into tears and fled to the nursery where Nanny comforted me and explained what drunkenness was!

Evidently it did not shock Mrs. Murray too much because each year she took me, by myself, to the circus in Kelvin Hall, Glasgow. She had a Rolls Royce which swayed and swung about the Stockiemuir Road over the hill to Glasgow and it was always touch and go if I would get there before being sick. I longed to open a window but this was not allowed. We lunched somewhere most respectable, and then, by our two selves, went to the circus! We must have looked a curious couple and it certainly was difficult for me to pretend I was having a whale of a time.

During the Easter holidays at Buchanan I led a very social life. On most days there would be a party given by some of my friends in the neighbouring countryside consisting of games and dances. Tennis was very much in vogue, and being rather good at the game it was certainly the most popular afternoon as far as I was concerned. At Buchanan itself we used to have afternoon parties for Easter, the climax of which was a hunt for the Easter eggs my Mother had hidden in every nook and cranny in the garden and round the woods — some coloured hard-boiled eggs and some chocolate ones, hidden in the bushes and mossy banks, or tucked up in the forks of branches.

On warm hazy Spring days Father hired a boat from Alex McFarlane of Balmaha, and we invited friends to go for picnics on one or other of the islands on Loch Lomond. There was Inchcailleach, with its old oak trees wind-blown into frantic shapes and crowned, on top of the hill, with a few remaining Scots firs from the old Caledonian forest surrounding an old graveyard. Another island was Inchmurrin where yew trees, used to make bows in history, still stand. This island belongs to the Colquhouns of Luss. It always seemed to be sunny and warm, more open than Inchcailleach. It

was covered with wild flowers, and many birds nested there.

Of course, half the fun, as always, in a picnic like this, was collecting the wood to make the bonfire, roasting the potatoes and eating sausages off a fork, and running round amongst the flowers playing games.

Alex McFarlane's family went back in history as the hereditary boatman for the Montroses. Though so long as I can remember he acted as postman, taking the post to people who lived on the islands, which in winter demanded a lot of courage as the loch could be quite rough and extremely cold, he seldom missed his round. On returning from the picnic I always went up to see his old aunt, known as "Miss McFarlane of the Point", her cottage being on the point at Balmaha Bay. She had the most wonderful store of stories which really should have been written down, but I don't think they ever were. One, I remember, was about a daughter of one of the Dukes of Montrose, who had been forbidden to marry the young man she loved, which broke her heart. Most days she would ask to be taken out in the family barge rowed by eight oars, with seats covered in Graham tartan, and an awning of tartan. She would ask to be rowed the full length of the loch, and back, and Miss McFarlane said you could still hear the sound of the oars as the barge returned late at night, and see the dark silhouette against the moonlight as it slid back to its moorings. The poor lassie died of a broken heart, Miss McFarlane concluded.

6

MY GRANDMOTHER AND OTHER ANIMALS

"G O on, Kelpie! *RATS!*"
That was my introduction to my grandmother,
Mary, Duchess of Hamilton, the widow of the
12th Duke of Hamilton, my mother's mother.
When I was a few weeks old my mother, proud
of her latest product, took me to see my Hamilton grandmother who was living in Lamlash in the White House. Like
all babies, when they should be on their best behaviour they
scream, and I was no exception. Laid out on my grandmother's bed in my best long frock made of fine lawn and
banded with lace, I howled. Kelpie, my grandmother's collie,
cocked his head this way and that and wondered what had
arrived on his mistress's bed.

"Go on, Kelpie, *RATS!*" she said again. Luckily for me he
did not obey her instructions any more than usual. Mother
was so infuriated that she snatched me off the bed and left
the house to drive back to Brodick and the safety of Nanny
Breeze and the nursery.

My mother's father, the 12th Duke of Hamilton, had died
when she was a little girl of 11 years old, leaving his estates in
the hands of trustees. The title of Hamilton was entailed and
went to cousins so distant that we had a common ancestor in
1650 and nothing closer.

My grandmother thought the cousins should be left
Hamilton Palace and contents, and that Mother should have
the Isle of Arran and an estate in Suffolk – Easton – which
was sold before I was born.

Hunting and riding were my grandmother's passion. She

69

and Mother spent a great deal of their time in various parts of the country where famous packs of hounds hunted.

My Grandmother's two other obsessions were gardening and house decorating. This took care of quite a lot of the family fortune because she would buy a house, do it up with no expense spared, create the most lovely garden, and then move on to do the same again — not always at a profit. By the time I

Mother on her racehorse 'Irish Sea', 1930

was introduced to her and her collie dog, she had already created the beautiful garden at Dougarie, on Arran, and two houses on the Easton estate and Easton itself, and was about to move to a house in Herefordshire called Lugwardine.

For several years just after Christmas, Nanny and I were taken there with Southgate and the ponies, for Mother's hunting season. On these journeys, carriages were attached to the trains so that we did not have to change.

It was a fine house standing on a hill above the River Lugg with stables, a pig house and room for a few cows at the back.

Nursery routine went on much as it did at home.

However, while there, Nanny went for a few days' holiday to see the paragons of virtue, the Lloyds, who lived in the next county, and Mother came to sleep in Nanny's bed in the night nursery. One night, some time after we had both gone to sleep, I woke up to find a white, luminous figure standing close to my bed facing me, not that I can remember the face, but I knew that I was being watched. I was completely petrified and if ever my hair stood on end, it did at that moment. The figure stood watching me for quite a long time, but I was too afraid to scream, then slowly it moved away and disappeared by the wall near the fireplace. Once it had left, with one bound I leapt from my bed, landing on Mother's chest. She got such a fright she screamed, I dissolved into tears and sobbed and was quite hysterical. I knew nothing of ghosts in those days and I was not told till long after Lugwardine was sold that the old part of the house incorporated an old ruined convent, then the nursery wing. There had been a passage which continued exactly where I said the figure had disappeared. Apparently several people had seen a ghost in that particular room before.

Once, when Mother was away I suppose, joy of joys, I awoke one morning to find a litter of tiny pigs in the day nursery in a laundry basket. I was so excited about the pigs I do not remember how, or if, Nanny was "put out". My grandmother came up to instruct me how to feed the piglets from a baby's bottle, emphasising the importance of not muddling the piglets up and giving two portions of milk to one and none to the other. As they were fed I had to mark their backs with a blue crayon. Life was great fun during these days, but when Mother returned to find her youngest little afterthought living in a pigsty, her reaction was sharp and clear and my piglets disappeared. I was not even

encouraged to feed them in the pigsty. How empty the nursery was after they had gone.

In the garden my Grandmother placed inverted half orange skins, the juice of which had already been used, stuck on top of short sticks a few inches high. This was an old method of catching slugs which would go up into the orange. I was put in charge of these traps and each morning had to go round the oranges and empty the slugs into jam jars. She paid me my first wages! Perhaps a farthing per slug, I cannot remember. She also had traps out for moles in the garden and I used to do the rounds with her gardener, and learnt a lot about mole trapping, skinning and pelt curing.

Mother's hunters were stabled some miles away and on Sundays she would get the chauffeur to drive us over to see them. As you walked under an arch into the square, the horses' heads would reach over the doors — 20 fine hunters shining with good grooming and good health. They knew the routine too. Watson, their groom, waited for us with a long, white, spotlessly clean coat, his leather leggings and breeches and his bowler hat. In his hands a large round wooden sieve filled with scrubbed, sliced carrots. As my mother and he walked round the horses, slipping them the odd carrot, discussing any injury or illness, making plans for the future week's hunting, I would look and listen. I was half-way between Father and Mother. I loved horses like Mother but, like Father, I thought they were "dangerous at both ends and damned uncomfortable in the middle". Brusher, as Watson was called, was equally proud of all his horses, and when I spoke to him just before he died in 1977, his memory was living over the great days of hunting with the famous packs of hounds in England, and he spoke of horses.

"My horses", he always said — the horses "I" sold. His horses had been the smartest outfit at the meets, his horses

72

had the most stamina and were the fleetest footed animals and the best jumpers following these illustrious packs. I dared mention that perhaps my mother had had something to do with it, too, that she, too, had been smartly turned out and that she, too, had been a good rider and that she had a good eye for the country that she rode across.

"Well," he said, "Of course she had to be for a smart outfit like mine!"

Driving back from the stables to Lugwardine on a cold winter's night in a car with, of course, no heating and perspex windows that flopped about letting in the wind, and a collapsible roof that was not air proof either, was a freezing experience. We had a big flat metal container covered with carpet and filled with boiling water on the floor and plenty of rugs, one of which Mother would put right over our heads. Pretending it was a tent we would play make-believe tea parties on the way home, or tell stories.

CASTLES IN THE AIR

7

GOVERNESSES

AT Brodick the cold war continued between the staff and Nanny, which was the same as in all big houses because the rest of the staff felt that Nanny had the ear of the Lady of the House much more so than they did. When governesses arrived war was declared and I found myself sandwiched between the two warring factions. As far as Nanny was concerned we were given too much work to do and were too tired to eat our suppers. As far as the governesses were concerned we were incorrectly clothed to go outside for our exercises, or too spoilt, or something else.

I had a succession of well-meaning women who lasted but a short time, to teach me. Miss Olrick started my lessons. My mother's old desk was put in the schoolroom. It had a wooden seat with a rounded wooden shape in the back which could be raised or lowered to fit the arch of my back to make me sit up. 9 a.m. till 12 noon were the hours for lessons, then at twelve o'clock we took a quick walk before lunch at one o'clock, followed by a rest on the sofa when I had to read a book or occasionally the governess would read me the life of a musician, Mozart, Liszt or Handel, and play a record of his music. We belonged to a record club which posted the records to us like a library book and they were returned when I had heard them. Even now I think there could be no more sure way of killing someone's interest in music than the way it was taught. Art was taught in the same way. The life of the artist was read and sepia prints of him were studied.

When Miss Olrick left, the lessons remained the same because the system taught was P.N.E.U. The syllabus was set by P.N.E.U. and trials were written at the end of each term and sent to Headquarters and marked.

Miss Duncan followed Miss Olrick. She was younger and used to receive love letters which she had a habit of concealing in the school books and forgetting. It was absolute joy to rush and take them out of their concealment and read them after lessons when she had left the schoolroom.

I think my education in those early years was varied so as to give me every opportunity to have many interests, and also had a lot to do with my mother's theory that boredom was the sign of lack of intelligence, which is a perfectly logical remark.

I don't think, though, I would have minded lessons nearly so much if I had had my holidays and my Sundays to myself. I think I must have been born to be the original member of a schoolgirls' trade union. I also had to earn my 2/6d. a week pocket money by feeding the house dogs and puppies of which there were twelve, for a time. When I was older I had to arrange the flowers in the house. I mentioned to Mother that I did not think 2/6d. was enough to cover this and would like a rise.

"That's funny," said Mother, "I was just working out how much the cost of living has gone up, I could countercharge you for that if you like."

It did not seem such a good idea after all, then she made it clear to me that a family can only exist if it works as a team with each helping each and giving of their best.

There was no room for temperament either. If one arrived at the breakfast table with a sulky face one was asked to leave the room till one could come back less of a gloom spreader.

French holiday governesses arrived almost as soon as the

76

other governesses had gone. I built up a great resentment on these points. I never seemed free to do the things other children did, I seldom went to stay with other children and they seldom came to my home. The French governesses were worse than the English ones. They hated having to play tennis with me, they were sick on the fishing boat and I adored the sea and boats, and of course the governesses would not bathe and they did not like riding.

I wonder if I was just stupid or the lessons were taught badly, or even if I had a touch of dyslexia which was a word unknown at that time. Whatever the reason I was extremely slow to learn and would often read a word backwards or even read the second word in a sentence first. Clocks I usually read back to front as a small child.

Then Miss Humphrey arrived, my new governess. She may not have been a great educationist but she gave me interests that have lasted me all my life. She stayed longer than any of the others. I was very good at handicrafts and made many yards of pillow lace. When she arrived she brought with her a very old pillow which was a round padded pillow with two short wooden handles which fitted into a padded frame. Onto this was pinned a thick paper band with perforations pierced according to the pattern to be followed. Pins were stuck in the perforations to hold the threads which were long and at the bottom end of each thread was a bobbin. Miss Humphrey's bobbins must have been extremely old and were made of decorated ivory three or four inches long with one or two little coloured glass beads at the end of each.

Basketwork was another handicraft and raffia work; I made felt animals and did Italian quilting, also a gros point seat for a dining room chair, during which time my grandmother made three, but she was a very quick worker of great experience. I have some of her canvasses which I am still

My Governess, Miss Humphrey, who was keen on Racing

working on and I find people today amazed that the pattern is a black outline only. With her threads she coloured her pattern as one might with a paint brush. If a leaf is required to look as if it turned over, the turn and the underside of the leaf had to be done by changing the wools. As a little girl she showed me how she did it and though I am nothing like the artist she was I have done a bed head and three seat covers of her set.

It is not from lack of trying that I am no good at drawing. At least one period each week was set aside for drawing and it was Mother's wish that I started at the beginning and worked till my basic drawing was correct before I lifted a paint brush. She herself had won medals for drawing when she was a girl and had gone to an art school. She painted in water colours as well as being a good sculptress. There were white wooden forms in the schoolroom and one of these would be put on the table in front of me, a sphere, a cube, a triangle or a crescent, and from these I had to learn shading and perspective. Only after a lot of work was I allowed to meet Mr. Stewart Orr, a famous water colour artist who lived in Corrie, who was good enough to come to the castle to teach me about mixing colours and colour washes. After a lot of practice Mother and I went out with him on the hills to sketch. I loved these days and he was good at imparting his great knowledge. Always dressed in a kilt, he was a most amusing companion and I still recollect my envy and disbelief that anyone could produce such pictures so quickly.

Little girls were seen and not heard and there was no interrupting grown-up conversation. I was apt to sink back into a day dream at the dining room table. Suddenly there would be a slap on the table and Mother would say,

"Humpy darling!" and I, (and the guests, often as not) would sit up straight. Slouching was forbidden as slackness

indicated a slack mind!

Miss Humphrey became a good friend of mine and a great friend of Nanny's. She made my walks interesting, collecting and naming wild flowers or watching wild birds. She rode with me in the afternoon and peace reigned between the schoolroom and nursery. In fact, to my surprise, while I was doing my prep in the evening, Nanny visited the schoolroom.

Miss Humphrey and she would sit side by side on the sofa reading the newspaper and I saw nothing unusual in their talk of Epsom and Newmarket, Gordon Richards, Steven Donague, and Harry Wragg. Gradually I learnt the names of horses, their breeding and their owners, jockeys and trainers and learnt quite a lot, too, about the betting odds and the bookies and thought nothing of it. It was part of my life for about six years, until one terrible day when my mother was giving a lunch party and I was having my lunch with the grown-ups in the dining room. They were talking about some big race due to be run the next day. They got mixed up as to which jockey was to ride which horse, and also the sire of one of the horses. I could stand their foolishness no longer so my childish voice piped up:

"Actually you are completely wrong," I corrected them.

There was complete silence round the table which I took to mean the grown-ups were interested in what I had to tell them and pressed on with the facts of the races, and the pedigree of some of the horses, and who was to ride them. Then I caught the horrified look on Mother's face and coldly she said,

"You seem to know a lot about racing. Where did you learn it all?"

I realised my mistake too late and stumbled to cover up for Nanny and Miss Humphrey, but really there was nothing I could do. I did not realise how seriously Mother would take

such a thing and that both the Montroses and the Hamiltons had lost their family fortunes in gambling.

By the next term a new governess had been found for me and Nanny was retired to a cottage in the park at Brodick where she lived with an old retired cook of my grandmother's, and the two old ladies fought many a good fight.

8

LIFE AT BRODICK CASTLE

FTER the First World War Mother felt that one central memorial for the dead in the shape of a hospital would have tremendous benefit for the people of Arran but she met with great opposition from all the villages who wanted their own memorial stone for the soldiers of their own villages. After many meetings a compromise was reached and it was agreed that each village would have its own small memorial, dignified though simple, and that each village would also raise money for the central War Memorial; and, in the end, the Isle of Arran War Memorial Hospital at Lamlash was built.

To raise money on an island with a small population of 4,000 was not easy, and in fact could not have been done without the great generosity of many of the summer visitors. She managed to get many well known artistes to come and give high quality concerts or Repertory Companies to produce plays in the summer. Not only did she build the hospital, but for years had to make enough money to keep it running until the National Health Service took it over. It has, of course, been a godsend to the island.

She had experience herself about the need for more doctors on the island and for a hospital. When she was a little girl at Dougarie she pushed her arm through the nursery window, cutting the artery. The only doctor was in Brodick, twelve miles away, and the only transport was by wagonette. Her life was saved by my Hamilton grandfather's Algerian valet Eduard, who packed the wound with black pipe tobacco (twist) which had a cauterizing effect, and stopped

My Father and Mother laying the foundation stone for the War Memorial Hospital, Lamlash

the bleeding during the long drive over the hill.

For all illnesses people had to go on the long, cold journey by sea and train to Glasgow, and many lives must have been lost from the inability to get medical attention quickly. Country people in isolated places take illness much more philosophically than townspeople.

Mother's interest in nursing and also in the welfare of the people of Arran made her realize that a hospital and a good doctor service was essential for the island.

A lot of people were frightened of Mother, and there is no doubt she was a great disciplinarian. We were brought up in her belief that privilege breeds responsibility and that one must "do your duty whether it is convenient or not convenient". How often have I had those two sentences rammed down my throat, as well as "each human being and each animal have their own dignity so treat them so".

I was never frightened of her — well, not often — but she could give the most imperial rows, which took the form of asking questions so that in giving your answers you would convict yourself. I would get a message, "Her Grace will see you in her Boudoir after breakfast" — that meant big trouble. I would open the door and she would be standing with her back to the fireplace. Of course, I was not offered a seat. In fact, I clutched the high-backed lug chair near the door and she would start,

"Why did you do such a rude or such a hurtful deed?"

Well, why does a child do anything? The answer was,

"I don't know."

"You must know. You cannot go through life not knowing what or why you do things. Are you proud of what you have done?"

Of course, standing there clutching my chairback I was proud of nothing so the answer was "No" and so it would proceed. If the offence had hurt anyone I would be sent to apologise or, if it was a serious offence, she would come with me to make sure I did apologise.

It wasn't only the children who got this treatment. In the Second World War 8,000 men from the Commandos were stationed in Arran, when they were first formed. The estate was bound to produce a certain number of deer carcasses for the Meat Marketing Board and to Mother's great annoyance, and indeed the keeper's great annoyance, a lot of these young men, away from the discipline of their own regiments and not yet having built up the *esprit de corps* of the

My Mother

My Father

Commandos, went on the rampage with anything from automatic rifles to revolvers, shooting at the deer. Twenty wounded beasts were found in the five miles between Brodick and Corrie. My father was away at the time. Nothing daunted, my mother sent a message to the Brigadier, saying,

"I would like to see you in my Boudoir after lunch."

He arrived, I am quite sure thinking he was going to be offered a nice glass of brandy. Instead, before he had time to take a seat she said,

"If you are unable to control your men here on the Isle of Arran how do you propose to do so if you get sent out to North Africa?"

By that night every officer in every platoon had a directive that if anyone was found shooting at any game they would be returned to their regiment.

When he returned my father was horror-stricken at what she'd done and said,

"Really, Molly, you cannot do this sort of thing to a Brigadier in the Army!"

"Well," she said, "I only asked him a perfectly civil question!"

My brothers and sisters found the discipline of the house very restricting. For some reason my mother never approved of their going out in the evening after dinner, so they would wait until everybody was in bed, change back into their tweeds and let themselves out through the skylight of the menservants' lavatory. They would then run down to the shore and go out in a boat, or bathe or something. The difficulty was to get back in through the skylight. The men would help the girls up onto the roof and then help them slide through the skylight over the water cistern, and down onto the lavatory, back into the house. Unfortunately one night the top of the cistern had been removed. One of the men tried to get in first, but slipped and fell with his bottom in the cistern and his legs flaying the air! Nobody was able to reach him to help for a time, and when they did, it required a lot of pulling and pushing before they finally got him out of the cistern and themselves in through the skylight! Unfortunately I was too young to join in these frolics.

My mother was very concerned about fire, and at least once a year a Fire Inspector came from the mainland in a very smart uniform to drill the house staff on the procedure if fire broke out. The fire escapes were tried out and people who slept in various parts of the house had to go down them. From the top floor where the housemaids slept — the part built for Cromwell's troops — there was a chute made of white canvas. At the start of the exercise the Fire Inspector would hold the bottom of the shute so that the maids would not come down too quickly. There were great screams of laughter as this went on. Trousers for women were not known in those days so as the girls landed there was a flurry of white petticoats and legs; but by the end of the exercise any one of the girls was proficient enough to control her fall with no-one holding the end, and then she would be able to help the others down. In the front bedrooms there were belts on long fireproof ropes. In the long distance of 125 feet from the tower to the ground these ropes unwound so slowly the belt nearly broke one's ribs, and I am sure we would have been burnt to a cinder in a real fire.

Apart from her sense of duty and discipline, Mother was the kindest, most gentle soul, with a wonderful sense of humour. I think it really was her shyness of people caused by her mother's sheltering that made her seem so distant. I am sure it was shyness that made her make some caustic remarks, really meant as a joke, but it often struck near the bone. The other side of her character far outweighed the

rather stiff picture I have painted. If anyone was in need of help or was ill, Mother would be the first to help, and there were many who mistook her generosity and played on it.

In the evenings when she was at home, after my nursery tea I would go down and play in the drawing room with her and any guests who were there or perhaps she would read to me some of my favourite books, amongst which were Beatrix Potter, Tarka the Otter, Black Beauty, Morland Mousie the Exmoor pony, and Winnie the Pooh. At other times we would play a game of skittles. The skittles were the most beautiful models of Turkish soldiers, and you knocked

Myself on Brodick Beach

them down with round wooden discs with a Turkish flag on them. I imagine these must have been fashioned at the time of the Crimean War.

We played Pelmanism, and on one occasion we built card castles which got quite high. I think Mother blew at them and they fell down so that I sat back on my heels and said "Damn you". Where I had learnt the word from I do not know, but the result was electrifying! I realised if one wanted attention from grown-ups one simply had to say "Damn you" which I learnt was called a swear word and so "little big ears" soon collected quite a few words, though I did not use them in front of Mother again! This scene is so set in my mind, I can still see the drawing room with the big fire burning, the marble mantelpiece, and being pulled to my feet by a very cross Mother, who led me back to the nursery. Nanny was questioned as to where I had heard such a word. It was decided that while my brothers were back for school holidays I must have heard it from them.

9

MONACO

N 1928 when I was aged 8, the whole family were invited to Monaco by Mother's cousin, Prince Louis de Monaco. A softly spoken, kindly giant of a man, he had twinkling eyes, greying hair, bushy eyebrows and a neat moutache and was a great favourite with us children, indulging our every whim.

His only child, Princess Charlotte, small, dark, very French to look at, smart and lively as a cricket, lived in an apartment in the Palace with her husband, Prince Pierre de Pollinac. He was always well groomed but rather distant as far as the nursery was concerned.

I remember little of the journey out there. Perhaps there were so many new things around me that I have no impression left, except that Nanny was seasick before the ferry boat had cast off from shore and that we travelled by train via Paris.

When we arrived at the Palace I met Prince Louis's grandchildren, Princess Antoinette, known as 'Tiny', a month younger than me, and her brother, Prince Rainier, two years younger. He was later to marry Grace Kelly, renowned for her beauty but who should be equally renowned for her serenity, depth of vision and wisdom. She has the same gift as our own beloved Queen Elizabeth, the Queen Mother, of making you feel you are the one person they wish to speak to.

I made friends for life. Tiny is like a sister to me and is one of those friends that never alter. I think we were rather nasty to Rainier because he was younger and we expected him to fetch and carry for us and do all the dirty work. Tiny and I

were both overweight and slow. He was thin and like a bit of quicksilver, never still for a moment.

Their English Nanny, Miss Wanstall, a Norland nurse, ruled supreme in their apartments which overlooked the Square in front of the Palace. They had their own footman, dressed in the Palace livery, to wait at table, called Michel, and a maid for the rooms. The two nannies got on from the start like old friends and gossipped away together for hours about other people's nannies and other well known families. The gossip was international, one could say — Nanny would refer to other nannies by the name of the family they worked for, so in Britain you got "Nanny Montrose" or "Nanny Hamilton" and abroad the same thing applied.

Tiny and Rainier had the most wonderful toys: big cars with pedals in which we raced each other up and down the garden terraces, a sand pit, and toy guns to play cops and robbers. We were taken to the Musee Oceanique to see the world renowned collection of fish and shells started by Prince Louis' father, Prince Albert, great-aunt Mary's husband.

Sometimes we walked down the huge length of steps leading from the Palace to the town to have tea and very rich cakes in one of the patisseries.

One afternoon a week we attended a matinee of the Ballet, or sometimes the Opera. It was there where Tiny taught me to sing to the music of *The Soldiers' Chorus*, from Faust:

> *Oh, Jemima, look at your Uncle Jim*
> *He's in the water learning how to swim.*
> *Now he's doing the breast stroke,*
> *Now he's doing the side*
> *Now he's under the water*
> *Swimming against the tide.*

By then there would be a karate chop from one or other of the nannies who sat behind us in the Royal Box. Sometimes

Palais de Monaco

Gallerie d'Hercule

they looked as if they were asleep.

"Just shutting the eyes", they said, "to enjoy it better, dear."

Sweets would be handed out to keep us quiet but in order to eat these and not be seen by the public we had to sink down behind the impressive gold balustrade which surrounds the Royal Box, resplendent with gold furniture and red plush curtains, carpets and upholstery. When I went as a grown-up with Prince Rainier and Princess Grace I was to think back to these days with fondness.

On my first visit I had gone with Tiny and Rainier to their dancing class which was very different to the one I attended at home. In Scotland from Buchanan Castle, dressed up in my best dress and velvet cloak, I drove with my governess to Miss Webster's class at Helensburgh where great emphasis was laid on deportment, the correct way to sit and walk. The boys were seated on one side of the room and the girls on the other and the boys were shown how to walk across the floor, bow to the girls and ask them to dance. We learnt the basic steps of foxtrots and waltzes there. In Monaco, with Tiny and Rainier I entered a room with about 20 French-speaking children, I was unable to speak the language and did not know a soul, and was instructed in expression through movement. We were told to act as butterflies or falling autumn leaves or the flames of a fire. The French children had been brought up to this but I had never seen such a thing before and felt clumsy in the extreme. I was completely unnerved by the experience.

At Easter there was a big parade through the town of Monaco, the Battle of Flowers, where floats entirely covered in flowers paraded round the streets. One was an Easter egg covered in daffodils, with a child dressed up as a little yellow chicken. The Palace Coach was a dome-like crown covered

Ronald and myself in fancy dress in Monaco

Bathing at Antibes. Left to right:
Angus, Mary, Tiny, Rainier, Nanny Breeze, Nanny Wanstall

Prince Rainier and Princess Antoinette in the garden of the Palace, Monaco

in white carnations.

Next day in the Palace they had a childrens' fancy dress party. I was dressed as a Spanish girl with a white lace mantilla and a big tortoiseshell hair comb, but the *piece de résistance* was my brother Ronald, who dressed as a young girl and went outside the Palace and entered with the other guests. He was beautifully made up and Prince Louis and his son-in-law Prince Pierre de Pollinac, kept quizzing us as to the identity of the beautiful young lady was that we seemed to know so well and were quite annoyed when they discovered that they had been fooled.

After tea we had a treasure hunt throughout the Palace for coloured Easter eggs but Tiny and I got a little bored with it. So we went off into the Throne Room which was not open to the rest of the guests and there we sat in perfect comfort on the throne, shelling and eating our eggs, hiding the shells under the seat. Unfortunately we were missed by the nannies who started to search for us and discovered us with a little pile of shells under the throne — they were not at all amused! We were both upbraided and sent to join the other children.

Our parents arranged that we should meet in London a month or two later at the house we had near Prince's Gate during the London season when my sister Mary was a debutante. Sadly, I was ill and did not see them till they came to Arran a month later.

My illness was blood poisoning. I had been staying with my mother in the country at the home of my uncle, Lord Malise Graham. Unfortunately his two sons and I had gone into the kitchen garden and had pulled and eaten some baby carrots just roughly washed under the tap. I'd had a tooth extracted the day before I went there, and it was thought that I got blood poisoning by dirt getting into the socket. Anyhow I was taken off to a London hospital by ambulance and was very ill indeed.

Poor Mother sat in my room each day and tried to read to me but the only thing I would listen to was G. F. Bradby's *The Flowing Tide:*

> *Do you hear the noise of waters as they*
> *hiss along the sand?*
> *Do you smell the salt sea-breeze again*
> *that rushes to the land?*

As I lay in a hot hospital bed I could think myself into the poem and smell and hear the sea at Brodick. The second poem I would listen to was James Hogg's *A Boy's Song* — *'Where the pools are bright and deep...'*. She must have been driven to despair by the repetition, but if she was, she did not show it.

When I had more or less recovered, Nanny and I went home to Brodick, and Nanny Wanstall brought Tiny and Rainier to join me there. Goodness, it was fun to have two such kindred spirits to do things with. Tiny and I were terrible gigglers and the least thing would start us off. Looking back it seems the sun was always shining and the world was full of laughter.

10

SUMMER HOLIDAYS

HE visit became an annual event, usually with the whole family, sometimes Nanny Wanstall and the children only. The nursery routine went on as usual, the nannies gossipped, and we children rushed around. The most extraordinary aspect of their visits was that neither the nannies or the grown-ups realised that we three ran up the tower staircase at Brodick and out through a small window and down the fire escape ladder to play houses on the roof. We climbed up further ladders and looked down the chimneys and threw pebbles down them, or ran along the battlements and in through a door that led to the maids' bedrooms where the maids would play their gramophone records to us — delicious romantic love songs, Hawaiian songs, tangos and foxtrots. The fact that we went to play in the maids' rooms was discovered and stopped at once, but no-one enquired how we got there and for summer after summer we played on the roof.

One of the French governesses I had in summer overlapped the Monacos' visit. They were as fed up with the poor soul as I was. While playing on the roof one day we heard her call to us from the lawn below us.

"Go on," said Tiny, "say blank blank blank". I shouted it out then we ran along the battlements to the other end of the castle. The governess was furious.

"Go on," they said, "say this and this and this". The swearing really had a great effect on the governess.

"Go on!" they said, and "On!" they said, then the poor woman dissolved into tears and fled. We were well content.

Then we heard a deeper voice on the lawn.

"Jean, Tiny, Rainier! Come at once! I will see you in my Boudoir!"

Goodness, Mother gave us a row, what a row! We have remembered it ever since.

Sometimes Prince Louis and their mother and father, Princess Charlotte and Prince Pierre, came with their ladies' maid and their valet. It was rather like a flight of migratory birds arriving, the valet and the maid chattered in a foreign language exuding a delicious smell of scent which was not usual in Brodick as Mother didn't wear any. It was the first time I had seen wardrobe trunks — large leather trunks — and masses of other luggage.

Usually we stayed a week or so at Brodick and then we all moved over to Dougarie Lodge on the west coast of Arran. The ritual each year was that the staff moved over in the Studebaker which was still one of the very few cars on the island, in the morning, leaving only a skeleton staff at Brodick.

Father and Grandmother (now in her seventies, but very active) and the dogs, walked up Glen Rosa across the shoulder of Ben Nuis and down Glen Iorsa — about 14 miles of rough heather and bog. The Studebaker returned to collect Mother and her guests. The nannies, Tiny, Rainier, myself and Southgate, fitted into the pony trap and off we drove.

It was easy going down the front drive but when we got out of the drive gate and turned right onto the String Road (which divides the island in two) the hill was too steep for poor Victory to pull a full trap up, so Tiny, Rainier and I would have to get out and push from the back, while Southgate led Victory.

The two nannies, in their large straw hats to shield their

eyes from the sun, sat in state. The first mile was not too steep and was sweet scented with gorse bushes, still with some bloom on them, and the hedges with great patches of honeysuckle ('honey-cockle' my grandmother called it for some reason, so honeycockle it was for me). We plodded up, pushing for all we could, up under the birch trees, up till the heather and the bog myrtle started, up and over the first bridge, the only one that was straight, for the others were curved to prevent the witches from crossing them as was the belief in all West Scotland. Then we got to the really steep part and even the nannies had to get out and walk. Nanny struggled on, the wind catching her grey dress which billowed out over her black laced boots.

The curlews hovered and called their tremulous call, and the air was sweet with the scent of heather. There is a deer fence down at the bottom of the glen running parallel to the road which my mother had erected to keep the deer to the north end of the island away from the best agricultural land in the south. From the String road we looked across the glen to the other side of the fence and could see the deer grazing. They are mostly hinds and calves on these hills in summer. The stags come down from the hilltops later in September.

It was a long climb for young legs, about 2 miles to the top where we all re-embarked and rode down on the far side. The sun was bright and before us across the moor lay Kilbrannan Sound, sparkling and inviting, and beyond were the rolling hills of the Mull of Kintyre sheltering us from Atlantic gales in winter and framing this idyllic scene in summer.

We clip-clopped down the hill and across Machrie Moor to Mrs. Weir's shop close to the sea. We always stopped there to see Mrs. Weir and her husband, Charlie. It was a typical shop such as was to be found in every rural area of Scotland. It had

Dougarie Lodge

a post office counter, all the necessary foods such as flour, butter, bacon and sugar, all the necessary everyday equipment such as fly papers, tin tacks, buckets, staples (wire was kept out at the back and so were a few tools), but on the shelf straight in front of the door with the bell which clanged every time it opened, was a row of large glass jars full of the most gorgeous coloured sweets, real gobstoppers, treacle brittle, 'strippet ba's', humbugs and lots of others. After our efforts of pushing the trap uphill and an afternoon in the fresh air we were allowed to spend our pocket money at Mrs.Weir's. We could not dally long. We had still to finish our journey to Dougarie which was a further mile or so along the shore.

From Mrs. Weir's we could see the white Lodge standing back from the shore, the walls outside covered from top to bottom with stags' antlers. It was a house full of a lovely atmosphere, a happy house, a lovely, ugly, old house. The

front of it was very Victorian, a typical Scottish shooting lodge, all eves and valleys and gables and verandahs, pointed mullioned windows and pointed doors. Some architect's dream, I suppose, and the tradesmen's delight because by its very nature the annual repairs were terrific!

Dougarie had been the family's favourite house for the autumn from and including my Grandfather Hamilton's day. Brodick Castle had been let for the shooting season and the family had always lived for two months at Dougarie. It was an ideal sporting estate where a rough average of 1,000 to 1,400 brace of grouse were shot over pointers each year, the stalking was good and in wild country, there were black game in abundance, snipe and, later on, a lot of woodcock. Within a hundred yards of the Lodge was a sporting little fishing burn, and a mile and a half up the glen, Glen Iorsa, a small loch with a boat for fishing. A five minute walk took us to a small sandy bay where we children bathed. At the end of the drive was a large boathouse divided into three areas, in one of which quite large boats could be winched up iron railings from the sea and kept in safety because the anchorage is very exposed.

However, the centre section of the boathouse had been made into a gaming room in my grandfather's day where the gentlemen retired after dinner. There was a billiard table, skittles and various tables of gambling games. My grandfather had been a friend of Prosperi who drew caricatures under the name of 'Lib' for the magazine of the day, *Vanity Fair*. He had been a guest at Dougarie and had drawn caricatures of my grandfather's friends, including the great sportsman, Sir John Astley, on the walls. Each caricature depicted an animal or bird with the head in the likeness of one of the guests.

It was to Dougarie that King Edward VII came and stayed

on several occasions, and he attended the sheepdog trials at Machrie in the company of Commander and Mrs. Keppel, Princess Victoria and Mr. A. Chamberlain. The Machrie Sheep Dog Trials were started by my grandmother and there is still discussion as to whether Machrie or Cumnock was the first Scottish Sheepdog Trial Committee formed.

The inside of Dougarie was, again, very Victorian. The hall and passages and stairs were panelled shoulder-high with deer skins, the stick racks were deer antlers, so were the door knobs. Most of the bedrooms were pine-panelled. There was no electricity till the Second World War and cleaning oil lamps was a daily chore for the maids. The drawing room has a window over the fireplace with the chimney going up inside the wall each side of the fire so while warming oneself one can stand and watch the changing lights on the hills either side of Glen Iorsa.

The west side of Arran is more sparsely populated than the east and in the days before cars people had a long way to walk to shop or to go to Church and the children a long sea-blown walk to school. Even today it is far less spoilt and wilder than the east of Arran. As late as 1928 there was no tarmac on the roads and the bridge over the burn was a narrow wooden one. If the burn was not too full most carts and traps went through the ford and the pedestrians over the stepping stones, which was a little shorter than going by the bridge.

The first evening at Dougarie, after tea, Tiny, Rainier and I were left on our own to explore. The favourite place was up into the garden which my grandmother had built. For a retaining wall 20 feet high she built a mock ruined castle against the steep hillside and inside this she had brought in enough soil to form a terrace almost to the top of the wall. Roses climbed up the 'ruin' and the beds were full of flowers.

At one end was a steep grass bank where we took tin trays and spent hours sliding down, or else we went up another flight of steps onto the second terrace and up more steps to the kitchen garden where the fruit grew — raspberries and gooseberries and plums — and eat to our hearts' content.

Despite the mock castle walls, the garden is very exposed. To the south west on a fine day, looking past Sanda Island, the tip of Ireland is visible, and to the west, Campbeltown and Carradale. The north east view is Glen Iorsa which stretches up to the foot of Ben Nuis on one side and Sail Chalmadale on the other.

Mr.Mathieson was the head gardener, a friendly giant with a burring speech who was always pleased to have a chat and a laugh. He kept the garden and the hedges so beautifully, despite the fact that we were there only two months in the year. On entering the kitchen garden, the path — all of 50 yards — was lined with the old fashioned Pinks called 'Mrs. Sinkins' which is so hard to buy today, and which smells so beautifully of cloves. Behind them was a line of a very tall catmint and then a hedge of roses of all colours. The vegetable plots were behind the roses and, despite the salt-laden gales and the rain, Mathieson produced some of the best vegetables of any of the Arran gardens. Dougarie for Tiny and me means the smell of Mr. Mathieson's pinks and the sound of the red-throated divers as they flew over the house up Glen Iorsa to their nests or down to the sea for their food.

Mr. Mathieson and his wife and crippled son, Murdo, lived in the little cottage by the shore at the foot of the drive. His son had been damaged at birth and was unable to hold his head up without supporting it in his hand. I am sure that with the advanced medicine we have now it would be almost a routine matter to mend this defect. To a child, however, he

was a frightening sight as his carriage made him look hunch-backed and his voice was muffled. It was not till I was very much older and had had quite a lot to do with disabled people that I got to know him and found that he was one of the best-read men you could wish to meet. He was also very sociable and loved going out to his neighbours. In the days I speak of I used to try to avoid meeting him but every morning and every evening I would watch Murdo exercise all the pointer dogs from the kennels. He walked through the arch at the kennels, down past the Lodge with ten or twelve pointers mostly coupled in pairs and a long leather whip in his one hand, his face being held up by the other hand. Usually one whistle and the dogs obeyed: if not, he only had to crack the whip in the air and they would race back to him. As there were no cars on the road he could walk them along the shore road for a couple of miles or more to the north and in doing so would pass some plots of potatoes growing on nothing more than shingle with seaweed used for manure.

These plots were ground leased to the famous potato breeder, Mr. McKelvie, who lived on the east side of Arran. He crossed potatoes, sometimes by pollination, sometimes by grafting, and grow them at first near his house in Lamlash village. When they had increased he distributed them to plots in different types of soil on Arran. After that he would send them to plots he leased all over Britain. For many decades his potatoes, *Arran Banner, Arran Pilot, Arran Chief*, to mention but a few, were household names and he made a lot of money. Then things went wrong for him and old age crept on. Once again he bred a potato that looked like a winner and everyone was delighted. Next we heard he had been offered a staggeringly large sum of money by one of the seed houses for his new potato. To the amazement of us all, it became known he had turned down the offer. One small plot of potatoes in the south of England had shown signs of disease and, honest man that he was, he would not sell them as a disease-resisting crop; a few months later he died, almost bankrupt.

Further along the Imachar shore Murdo Mathieson and his dogs walked past the smallholding where John Sillars and his sister lived. "Seonaidh Leasbuig", as he was known, was an old man when I first knew him. When one is eight all grown-ups seem to have one foot in the grave, but he really was old. He had never changed his looks to keep pace with fashion and still sported a very striking beaver beard; his right eyelid drooped and on his head was a "fore-and-aft" in tweed that matched his plus fours, with a big ribbon bow on top of his head tying the ear flaps up. He always walked with a large shepherd's crook and wore black dubbined "tackety boots" with the toes turned up and a good pair of hand-knitted stockings.

Seonaidh Leasbuig had acted as ghillie to the family all his working life and had done odd jobs around Dougarie when he was not working on his smallholding. I think curiosity was his main driving force. Within a few days of the family moving to Dougarie he would appear — "Just passing by, ye ken" — and would make sure he met my mother to find out who was coming to stay and when, and pass the time of day with her. He must have been the keeper's nightmare because it seemed as if he watched which hill they were stalking on, day by day, and he must have watched every move, because no sooner would a beast be shot than Seonaidh would materialise from behind a rock "Just passing by, ye ken" and would look at the dead beast with scorn in his voice that had never cracked properly and therefore jumped from the high pitch of a boy down to a very deep gravelly voice of a man. He would stand, hand on crook, and come out with some disparaging remark,

"Losh! Losh! Man, yon's an awfu' wee beastie to ask a chentleman to shoot", or "My, my, it took you a fair time to get into yon wee staggie".

If they were shooting grouse then there would be some comment that the dogs were not as good as in his day or the hill was not as well kept.

There are plenty of stories about the old man, but one that passed into legend was when he was out stalking with my grandmother who was, as custom dictated, wearing a long Shetland-knitted skirt down to her boots because to show an ankle was considered shocking. The Duchess had to negotiate a deer fence and decided that to go through between two strands of wire would be safer than to climb the eleven strands. She got hooked up and shouted to Seonaidh to help her.

"Am I nearly through the wire, John?" she asked.

"Dhia-gleidh mi, (Lord preserve me) you're all through, your Grace, nothing left behind but your arse."!

He only had a few sheep, but with great regularity won at least one class at the local show. Dark words were spoken among the various farmers and shepherds on the subject. One day two or three of them decided they would watch Seonaidh Leasbuig and his movements about the hills. There was a good lamb or two at Sannox on the east side of the island that year and Seonaidh had been seen in that area once or twice, "Just passing by, ye ken". Sure enough, one day not long before the show, he was seen leaving his smallholding early in the morning with a couple of his sheep dogs heading in the direction of Sannox, a long walk with only one pass where a man could drive sheep. So the other shepherds followed and lay in wait. In the afternoon they saw him coming with a ewe and a lamb, and just when he was about to pass them they leapt out of the heather. He saw them and looked round quickly. On one side was a steep cliff and he bounded off up the cliff throwing rocks down at the men, calling his dogs off the ewe and lamb and shouting some unprintable words at the men and then disappeared over the skyline.

By the time they reached the top of the cliff there was no sign of him and by the time they reached his cottage he was sitting in his chair in his slippers reading a book and no evidence that he had been out was to be seen. He greeted them like long lost friends and offered them a dram. That year he did not win the lamb class but instead won the best gimmer (yearling sheep) class.

Towards the end of his life he became very ill and the doctor warned his sister that the end could be expected. She started to lay in a store of whisky and shortbread and fruit cake so that those attending the expected funeral would want for nothing. The shroud was prepared and everything neatly stored in the cupboard. But Seonaidh's box bed was in view of the cupboard and he was not so far gone that his shrewd old eyes would miss a bottle of whisky. With impatience he waited for his sister to leave the house to milk the cow and feed the chickens. Somehow he mustered all the strength he had and slid onto the floor and crawled over to the cupboard. When his sister returned, there he was, propped up against the wall, with an empty bottle of whisky beside him. It did him the world of good and when my brother, Angus, called on him some time later he remarked on how well Seonaidh was looking and that he had heard he had had a dram or two. I think the old boy thought my brother wanted to share the whisky and, quick as a knife, said,

"Aye, but there's nane but the shroud left the noo."!

111

11

DOUGARIE

THE usual day's routine for Tiny, Rainier and myself was that we bathed in the morning. We ran ahead of the Nannies down the drive and over the stepping stones, hoping to heaven we didn't fall in because there was always a row when we did, despite the fact that we were going to bathe and would get wet anyway. The Nannies would leisurely wander down the drive, each carrying a wicker basket full of towels, bathing caps, bathing suits, the regulation thermos flasks of milk, and digestive biscuits, and they would have the key of the little bathing hut. While we played around they would get out the deck chairs and their knitting and ensconse themselves in comfort. We would undress and, in our bathing suits, play on the small patch of sand which is all that is available at Dougarie, unlike Brodick which had a mile of sandy beach. They would sit and chat while we built sandcastles and played around in the water. Finally we were more or less driven in to bathe properly to get wet all over. When we had got thoroughly cold, we would be called in and rubbed down with a rough turkish towelling which was bliss, and given a drink of hot milk and a digestive biscuit. Then we were sent for a run to get warm.

If the timing was right we would see Postie in his little trap drawn by a dun Highland pony coming round the corner at Mrs. Weir's shop and trot along the shore past the school. If we ran very fast we would catch up with him before he turned off the main road to the clachan of Auchencar. Occasionally he would be kind enough to give us a "hurl" in his trap which I think, from the Post Office point of view, was probably not

Prince Rainier, Princess Antoinette and me

legal, but it gave three children a memory for life. Having delivered the letters at all the little cottages and smallholdings at Auchencar he would trot across the moor and down the very rough road back to near the bathing box and cross the ford, allowing his horse to drink if it was a hot day, and then up the drive to Dougarie, so we arrived home before the Nannies' stately procession back to lunch.

In the afternoons. if it was fine, we went down to the boathouse and there I am not sure what we thought we were playing at but we imagined we had an industry of grinding sandstone by beating sandstone rocks with the harder granite stones and make mud pies. Nanny brought the picnic tea with her plus a little brown enamelled pan, white

114

enamelled on the inside, and we were sent with our pails to collect winkles off the shore. The winkles then had to be soaked in the fresh water which came down the Iorsa burn quite close to the boathouse and the fresh water made the winkles sick up the sand. After this we were sent to collect driftwood and build a bonfire and boil the winkles in the little brown enamelled pan. Then, sitting on the sun-warmed steps of the boathouse, with the Nannies in their wickerwork chairs from its porch, tea would be served. I have no idea if it is a childhood memory or if, in fact, no gourmet has ever written the recipe for the most delectable high tea for children: winkles freshly boiled, served with brown bread and cress sandwiches, the winkles taken from their shells with Nanny's hatpins. Maybe it was the sand in the sandwiches or maybe it was the sun-warmed steps or maybe Nanny's hatpin or magic in the little brown saucepan, but it was a gourmet dish.

One of the highlights of our two months at Dougarie was the Machrie Sheepdog Trials held on the Machrie golf course. Machrie is an area, not a village. Then, it consisted of Mrs. Weir's general store and two clachans, Auchengallon and Auchencar and a golf course. 'Golf course' is a very grand name for an area of cut grass, heather and bracken with a little wooden clubhouse with a tin roof. To this day it is still a place where many families with children of all ages have much pleasure in hitting a golf ball with a sparkling sea not many yards away and the hills shining in the sun behind them.

As I have mentioned, the Machrie Dog Trials had been started by my maternal grandmother. Originally they were held at Dougarie Lodge, but when they became bigger they were removed to the golf course. "Baldie" Craig was the secretary, and a very good host indeed.

115

There was a tent just the other side of the road from where we sat. People went in with rather long faces, and came out with much higher colour and invariably with a smile. As children we did not understand about the "little refreshment" that goes with all agricultural outings.

On the rough hilly field near the tent the main crowd sat on their rugs, dressed in their bright summer dresses and looking for all the world like a herbaceous border. From there they got the full view of the course. But the elite of Arran sat on their rugs on a bank against a hedge near the Judge's Table and very near the stand from where the shepherds started their dogs.

It was to Arran's disadvantage that the wealth of Arran was in the hands of so many spinsters who came from hardworking families who had made good. There were the eight Miss Allans, only two of whom were married, who were daughters of a well-known farmer who had made his money from pedigree Clydesdales and pedigree blackfaced tups (rams). There were the two Miss Fergusons whose father was a Master of sailing ships going to New Zealand, and whose great-uncles had made a fortune trading in Canada. There were two Miss Sweets, the daughter of the banker in Lamlash, one of whom married. And there were the four Miss Kerrs, daughters of the captain of my grandfather's yacht, two of whom married, there were two Miss McBrides who lived on the west coast of Arran at Shiskine, one of whom married. Their uncle had been one of the first directors of the Donaldson line.

In the days of sail all the ships went down the Kilbrannan Sound on the west coast of Arran to take full advantage of any wind from the west. Miss McBride had a charter permitting the members of the family to hoist a flag at Drumadoon Point near Shiskine which would indicate that

116

Nursery group at the boathouse, Dougarie. Myself, Tiny and Rainier with Nannies Breeze and Wanstall

they wished to board the Transatlantic ships to sail to Canada and the ships would stop and pick them up, though I don't believe this ever happened. These ladies, naturally wearing hats and gloves, and high lace collars, gold-rimmed glasses or lorgnettes or pince nez, would sit on their rugs close to my mother and father and Nanny Breeze and Nanny Wanstall, Tiny, Rainier and myself. The shepherds would come to the starting point, having received much hospitality from Baldie, and although I did not appreciate the language they were using, the effect on the row of these good ladies was reminiscent of swallows collecting on telephone wires before their migratory flight, they chirruped and clucked and exclaimed. Dan Bannatyne seemed to have the greatest effect, and one and all of the ladies would put a gloved hand to her mouth and face her neighbour and make suitable shocked remarks with many tut-tuts.

"Do you hear that?"

"Oh, my!"

"Is that not awful?"

"It's just terrible, tut, tut!"

The audience on the bank of the hilly field would go into guffaws of laughter, and the only living creature within sight who paid no attention was the dog to whom the remarks were being directed!

To us children it was a long sit and we welcomed the point when either Mother or Father were invited to present the cups and we could once again go home.

Just beyond the golf course was Machrie Farm, farmed by James Morton who had married Mary, one of the eight Miss Allans. We got an annual invitation to go and have tea at Machrie Farm and we got into the pony trap at Dougarie and clip-clopped along the Machrie shore to the farmhouse. After a little play in the garden we were invited to tea.

The Mortons were strict Free Church of Scotland members. We would be shown into the dining room where there was a large table, literally groaning with home-baked food — brown scones, white scones, treacle scones, *potato scones*, sponge cake, fruit cake, shortbread — everything you could imagine, home made jams and honey, jugs of creamy milk, but no-one could sit down until James had said Grace. But the Grace was no ordinary Grace, it told us that we really had no right to eat the food of the earth we were so evil, we really

had no right to take any pleasure in anything that tasted good, could we be forgiven, if we partook of the meal, and it went on and on for five minutes. Only then could we sit down and we really made the best of this most marvellous spread of food. After that we had to stand behind our chairs when a further thanksgiving was said lasting again for about five minutes, asking God's forgiveness that we had indeed partaken. Our manners had to be impeccable because anything at all slipshod would have horrified the Mortons. However, they were the most hospitable couple that you could imagine and we always enjoyed our afternoon there.

Other days, if the weather was fine we went for picnics to the Machrie river which is beyond the Morton's farm. Driving in the trap along the Machrie shore is a delight for anyone interested in wildlife. As the pony trap moved along the metal road there were many pairs of Oystercatchers escorting their young from the fields across the road, down to the shore, making their wild cry and their little chicks like balls of fluff running after their parents, their legs moving so fast they looked more like balls of wool self-propelled. There were Ringed Plovers and Sandpipers all guarding their territory with a lot of noise, Ducks and Divers and, of course, Cormorants. The rough area of grass between the road and the shore is covered with Harebells and Scotch Rose, Yellow Bedstraw, Silverweed and White Campion and the silver leaves of Mertensia among the rocks on the shore, and, of course, the smell of the Atlantic, so different from the shore smell on the Brodick side of Arran.

There were plenty of little blue butterflies, or "flutterbyes" as we called them. We progressed along the shore past Mrs.Weir's shop and past the golf course round the bend where we caught sight of the fishing hut standing on a high bank, a wooden hut with heather used for thatch, and a

At the fisherman's hut, Machrie. Nanny Wanstall, Rainier, Tiny, Ronald, me and Nanny Breeze

stone chimney. We went as far as the bridge and Victory was unharnessed. We ran along a footpath with a high bank on one side and the river on the other and Victory would follow us along. We each carried a jam jar of worms which Mr. Mathieson had given us, and we were met by the river watcher, Geordie Shaw, in plus fours and a shirt and his pork pie hat.

We only went there when it was fine, sunny weather, not ideal for a serious fisherman. Geordie Shaw showed us how to make up a rod and tie the line and the hook and how to put a worm on a hook, and we each were spaced along the river. Tiny and Rainier would catch little brown trout a few inches long amid enormous excitement. My own attention would

*Princess Antoinette on Machrie River. Geordie
Shaw and Prince Rainier in the background*

be caught by the sight of a Dipper bobbing up and down on a
rock, his white shirt catching the light, or in the cow parsley
on the other side of the river there seemed to be movement,
maybe shrews, maybe an otter. The flowers here were very
lush: Ragged Robin, Red Campion, Scabious, Speedwell,
Bugle Orchis, to name but a few. I fished by worm, and mine
used to float down and lodge amongst the stones and rocks,
so my main catch was eel. However, they gave me as much
excitement as a proper fish and usually by the time Nanny
shouted for us to go and have tea we had a sizeable catch of
fish which we fried up over the open log fire in the
fisherman's hut. Victory would then be caught as she grazed
in the field beside the bank and we wended our way back to

121

Geordie Shaw with Prince Rainier

Dougarie again.

A regular visitor to Arran was Cosmo Gordon Lang, Archbishop of Canterbury. He was a great friend of Mother and Father and had married them. He came very often and was a very good-looking and distinguished man who had the same charm as his brother, who later became Moderator of the Church of Scotland. The Archbishop had a face like Mr. Punch and blue twinkling eyes and he adored children.

One day when I went with my parents to fish on the Machrie river a lot further up the river than the fisherman's hut, the Archbishop and my father wished to get to the other side of the river. My father, who did not mind getting his feet wet, offered to carry the Archbishop on his back. My father had taken his shoes off to wade into the river and the rocks hurt his feet. Father said,

"I'm going to drop you, I am going to slip and fall!"

The Archbishop jokingly told him to be careful as he didn't want to go flat on his back in the river. Of course Father

started to laugh and the end result was that when they were almost on the far side my father really did slip but managed to pitch him onto the far side of the river bank where he landed on all fours looking rather like a large spider that has just hit the ground! He joined in so many of our ploys and was so very sweet to children that we all adored him, and looked forward to his visits, he had a wonderful sense of humour.

Another day when my parents were fishing in a very deep pool, Father, dressed as usual in his kilt, went to land a big fish which somebody had on their line. He slipped and fell in, and the air trapped under his kilt made it almost impossible for him to lean forward and swim. He went floating down the river like a top with his kilt like a ballet dancing skirt billowing out all around him!

One of our favourite sports was fishing for mackerel from our boat. My father had bought an extremely seaworthy boat built on the lines of an old fishing smack. We had a boatman, Hume, who had come from Campbeltown with his wife and a large family of children who lived in a cottage at High Dougarie near the Dougarie Farm just up the hill from the Lodge. We spent many hours in the boat. In the early morning we lifted the lobster pots which he had placed along the Imachar shore. And in the days I am talking about there was no question of 'over fishing', so we seldom lifted the ten pots without getting two or three lobsters and quite a number of crabs. If they weren't required at the Lodge for immediate use their claws were tied with string and they were put into a floating prison near the boathouse. No-one thought of stealing them.

The excitement of catching the rope marked by bobbing corks with the boat hook and pulling up the lobster pots, the cries of delight if there was something in it, our every-ready hands to rebait the pots ourselves meant we didn't in the

least bit mind the stinking old fish that were put in for bait. How happy these memories are.

After that we trolled lines behind the boat with coloured feather flies and could guarantee to get three or four different kinds of fish in quite large quantities. The nursery party monopolized the boat with our fishing trips and outings across the Kilbrannan Sound to Campbeltown or Carradale. Both were busy ports for the herring fishing fleets, mostly sailing boats, but a few of the new expensive motor boats would be there too, though rather resented by the sail fishermen who in no way could compete.

When we were not in residence, our boatman, Mr. Hume, was employed to do maintenance work about the place and keep the sea boats and the loch fishing boats scraped, varnished, and in good order. His wife kept Dougarie Lodge aired and polished. She had nine children when he died of cancer. She elicited the help of her deaf and dumb sister-in-law, Aunt Bessie, to baby-sit while she continued to work, and she held her family together. My mother brought them over to a cottage in Brodick where she continued with our family to augment her income and took on work as part-time cook. Most of her children learnt deaf and dumb language to be able to talk to Aunt Bessie. The eldest son, Peter, had to leave school early at 14 to bring another wage into the house and, in fact, he came with us as a carter to Buchanan. With the exception of a few years working for another Arran family he has been here ever since. In 1979 he received his long service certificate from the Scottish Landowners Federation at the same time as Duncan Langlands, who has been with my family all his life and is, in fact, the third generation to work here, covering about 100 years.

12

ARRAN IN WINTER

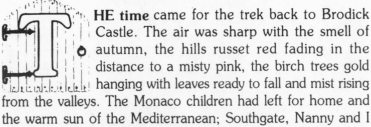

HE time came for the trek back to Brodick Castle. The air was sharp with the smell of autumn, the hills russet red fading in the distance to a misty pink, the birch trees gold hanging with leaves ready to fall and mist rising from the valleys. The Monaco children had left for home and the warm sun of the Mediterranean; Southgate, Nanny and I returned alone across the String Road in the pony trap to Brodick where we spent some weeks before moving to Buchanan.

By now the stags were down from their high summer grazings and across the glen on the other side of the deer fence they presented a panorama of grandeur. The hill An Tunna slopes steeply from the skyline to the burn running along the bottom of the glen, and the whole scene of stags during the rut is played out before your eyes. Great stags, the real Monarchs of the Glen, roaring and challenging each other to fight, rounding up their hinds, trying to steal another stag's hinds, chivvying and bullying. Often as not some small young stag that has been standing on the sidelines will nip in and drive the hinds away before the big boys realise what has happened. Then with a terrifying roar the old boy chases the young one away and gives him a punch he won't forget and regains his hinds.

Again Southgate and I walked up the hill to ease the load of the old pony, leaving Nanny sitting comfortably on her own. We stopped for a breather at the top of the hill. To our left across the moors with their wonderful autumn colours lay the whole range of granite mountains, Beinn Nuis, Beinn Tarsuinn, Beinn a Chliabhain and across Glen Rosa Goatfell

125

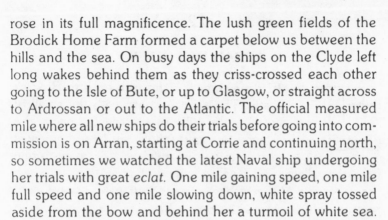

rose in its full magnificence. The lush green fields of the Brodick Home Farm formed a carpet below us between the hills and the sea. On busy days the ships on the Clyde left long wakes behind them as they criss-crossed each other going to the Isle of Bute, or up to Glasgow, or straight across to Ardrossan or out to the Atlantic. The official measured mile where all new ships do their trials before going into commission is on Arran, starting at Corrie and continuing north, so sometimes we watched the latest Naval ship undergoing her trials with great *eclat*. One mile gaining speed, one mile full speed and one mile slowing down, white spray tossed aside from the bow and behind her a turmoil of white sea.

Tourists had left by then, not that the tourist trade was anything like it is today. Most of the big comfortable boarding houses were built soon after the First World War and camping sites were unknown. Arran was almost entirely agricultural, but freight, both bringing agricultural manures and feedstuffs in and exporting live animals, makes farming extremely difficult. During the slump the estate reduced the rents of the farms to what they had been in 1881 to make life easier for the farmers. In the long run this action was very detrimental because as time passed the estate was unable to carry out the improvements and the repairs that had to be done and the rents were left low.

When the summer visitors left, as indeed happens now, the social life of Arran comes alive. In the 1920s there was very little social life, but my mother and my father worked hard to rectify this. She started the Scottish Women's Rural Institute in Arran and formed a Federation with nine institutes, one in each village, which, before the days of television and women's coloured magazines, fulfilled a need that can hardly be imagined today. It taught the women imaginative homemaking using their limited resources to the fullest possible extent, and it taught them new ideas in cooking, extending the limited food to nourishing dishes. Although there may not have been much money to get demonstrators to come over from the mainland, it wasn't very long before people of talent who lived locally were winkled out to pass on their knowledge to others. But quite apart from this more serious side the monthly meeting was one of the few social outings the women in isolated farms had to enjoy. The meetings were arranged to take place at the time of the full moon as the women had to walk to the village hall and back. The husbands did not seem willing to help out with transport, and indeed it would have been a lot of work to harness up the ponies and carts.

The formation of the Women's Institute coincided with Father's efforts to start a Drama Festival. Arran managed to produce anything between 20 and 24 teams competing in the One Act Play Section. Nearly every village institute entered a team as well as the British Legion and the other village teams.

To raise money to send the winners from Arran to compete on the mainland in the Quarter Finals my mother had a Fancy Dress Dance in Brodick village hall one year. Father said he didn't feel much like going and so she went off herself. A great assembly of people arrived in magnificent fancy dresses and the dance was in full swing when an old tramp bought his ticket and came in with a sheepdog on a piece of string for a lead. He had a red sweat rag round his neck and an old cloth cap on his head. He shuffled in and sat on the trestle seat near the door and soon took out an old clay pipe and filled it with tobacco twist. There was a great confab amongst the stewards as to how to get rid of the old boy because he had bought his ticket, he was perfectly sober and although the rest of the assembly moved away from him there was no noticeable smell. When he was asked to leave, he refused. It wasn't until the fancy dress parade commenced and the old tramp got up to join in that it was discovered that in fact it was my father!

By local efforts such as this the Arran drama teams were

Amateur Dramatics at Brodick.
A.K. Wooley, Mlle de Larabrie and my Mother

financed to go to the mainland and on many occasions brought honour to the island.

Also my mother started the Musical Festival. The first meeting was held in the castle in 1929 and the keenness shown by those who were asked to join the committee was such that Mrs. Shaw from Whiting Bay — a full 12 miles to the south of Brodick over two quite steep hills — walked the entire way on a dark winter's night to attend the meeting. When Mother discovered what she'd done she sent her home by car, but it showed unbelievable enthusiasm.

A talented musician herself, Mother recognized and appreciated talent in others. In the summer of 1924 when running a concert my mother heard a young Scoutmaster sing and admired his voice. He was, in fact, camping at Lamlash and she invited him quite frequently to sing for her at various functions. His name was James Montgomery Fyfe. Recognizing his tremendous talent, she asked if he would like her to help him train as a professional singer. This he agreed to do, and for a time sang in opera. Later he changed his name to Monte Rey and sang for Geraldo and Joe Loss's Band. Eventually he topped the bill at the Empire Theatre in Glasgow. 'The Donkey Serenade' was his signature tune.

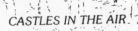

13

SPORTING LIFE

IN all estates, the Head Keeper stands slightly apart because he comes more under the jurisdiction of the owner and, on a long day stalking on the hill, becomes a companion. His interests are your interests, he is part of the countryside. The difference between Fraser at Brodick and Hardie at Buchanan was that Fraser was a stalker first and grouse and pheasant keeper second: whereas Hardie, who reared so many pheasants, was a low ground man first and only stalked a few red deer. They were different types of men, both expert in their own field.

Fraser was an outstandingly good keeper and ruled an empire of his own with a rod of iron. My mother told me that his father came from a well-known poaching family in Invernessshire and that the landlord on whose ground they operated wisely thought it would be a good thing to engage the sons as keepers so they could follow their love of sport legally instead of always being on the wrong side of the law!

As Head Keeper he was much respected by the rest of the estate workers and certainly rated only second to the Factor. He and my mother were one day walking from the castle up through the woods towards Goatfell when they passed a group of foresters who stopped in their work and said,

"Good morning, your Grace," and then turned to Fraser and said "Good morning, Mr. Fraser".

With his back hunched and his stocky frame set on his ultimate goal of the hill he walked on without acknowledging them.

Mother reprimanded him by saying, "Really, Fraser, when

these men say good morning to you as Head Keeper they are showing respect for your position and you should say good morning back again."

"Why should I?" he said, "I never speak to strangers."

My mother replied, "I presume Mrs. Fraser must have been a stranger at one time and you must have spoken to her."

"Aye," he said "and I wouldna' have done that if it hadna' been that I was made Head Keeper here with a muckle great house and I needed a housekeeper."

In fact, Mr. and Mrs. Fraser were a devoted couple and they lived their lives out in Arran, and died within six weeks of each other, in retirement, but he was not prepared to give way to Mother.

Fraser had a great sense of humour and had a great chuckle which one could see coming because his whole body shook and his eyes twinkled long before he laughed. He had short legs with the largest calves I have ever seen and in later life, as I puffed up the hills behind him, I would see those legs gaining and gaining ground in front of me. He would get so far ahead and then sit and light his pipe, but as soon as I reached him he would be up and off and the whole process started again. He had a very large back to his head and wore his cap perched on top of the crown and down to his eyes.

I was not the only one he would not allow to catch up with him on the hill. A story is told of when the famous artist, Balfour Brown first arrived in Arran to stay with my parents he made the fatal remark to Fraser,

"I hope you can walk, because I can."

That really was a challenge. They left the castle, ostensibly to look for stags to paint, but Fraser led him up Glen Rosa and on to Beinn Nuis, along Beinn Tarsuinn and A'Chir over to Caisteal Abhail and Sdoilan Im and along the ridge and down onto the Lochranza road and back through Corrie, a

Angus, Alex Fraser (Head Keeper) and Father

distance of some 22 miles. Someone in Corrie who saw them passing by in the evening said they were still walking as hard as they could go, and if one got in front the other would run some paces to get ahead and so on, all the way back to the castle.

Balfour Brown did a lot of his work here in Arran and as an old man rented Dougarie Lodge for many seasons for the enjoyment of his nephews and friends and spent many afternoons with Fraser in his retirement cottage. They were close and really lifelong friends.

Fraser and Mother went stalking one day and my mother was surprised at the route they took as it did not seem to go near the deer they had spied; but as Fraser did not appreciate conversation on the hill, one followed, unquestioning, to the end. Eventually they came to a big rock and there beside it was a line of spent bullets.

"Yon's Sir Vincent's (Sir Vincent Bradley) an awful shot yon," he said. He turned away down the hill again to get on with the stalk! On Sir Vincent's next visit he got a stag, and on meeting Fraser she said,

"Well, Sir Vincent got his stag, I hear."

"Aye, but it was no' the one he aimed at", was the only reply. One could never win!

One tremendous change since the turn of the century has been the acceptance of women on the hill either for shooting or for stalking. At one time it was considered a nuisance that the ladies drove out to join the guns for the lunch hour; that they should wish to walk with the guns or even follow whilst the stalk was in progress was anathema to the men, and women who expressed the wish to follow a shoot or stalk were considered "fast" in the extreme and a great bore. Even to this day they are considered a danger and a menace and are not really accepted as being capable of carrying a gun.

During the span of time that we speak of the fashion of clothes worn by women on the hill has changed out of all recognition. My mother told me a story of when she was young trailing around the Arran hills in a lined Shetland wool knitted skirt down to the ankles which caught on the heather and the bracken, and when wet was almost insupportable. Soon after her marriage she raised the hem to just above the top of her laced boots, but my father sent her back to change saying that the keepers would be horrified at seeing her ankles and boots.

134

Father on Arran with his beloved Bonny

I was 15 when I first went out stalking, and it had changed sufficiently for the women of the family to wear Plus Two breeches and thick woollen stockings and shoes, but over the breeches was a skirt to below the knees buttoned down the front. Only when crawling in to the stalk could one open the buttons down the front and pull back the flaps and button them onto the pockets, thus leaving your knees fairly free to crawl. My mother never went without this skirt and was rather scandalised when she discovered that I left the skirt with the man who was leading the Highland pony as soon as I got to the hill!

In her young day she had always worn a flannel shirt and tie, but in my day I was allowed to wear a woolly jersey. Her generation always wore a flat tammy, but in my young days I was allowed to go hatless.

Fraser was in charge of eighteen men, seventy pointer dogs, six or eight Highland ponies, the servicing of all the guns, rifles, game bags, panniers for the ponies, equipment in the bothies which housed the temporary ghillies, etc. etc. He arranged with the tenant farmers what heather they wished burnt in the Spring because the law to permit them to burn on their own did not come into force till the war when there were not men available to burn for them. Naturally he could not visit each tenant every year and relied on the beat keepers to make the arrangements on their ground. There were five kennels in Arran, though if things went wrong he had to take the blame.

Not that things were likely to go wrong with keepers such as David Reaside, who had been at Dougarie for years and years, and McHardy in the south end and McKillop on another beat. They were all first class men who knew their job as only experts can.

The kennels were beautifully maintained. The concrete

dog runs were scrubbed down each day, the grass runs scythed, and the iron railings round them painted with tar as a preservative. Thirty pointers were kept at Brodick and the remaining forty dogs distributed round the other shooting lodges. As well as pointers there were a lot of small black and white Springer Spaniels for retrieving and for the winter shooting. All the dogs were worked hard when the shooting season was in full swing. Only two, or at most three, guns went out with each dog handler, and three dog handlers were out each day on a different beat for six days a week with four pointers each during the grouse season. The same arrangements took place at each of the other lodges.

To get dogs fit enough to last the pace on Arran's steep hills took weeks of training beforehand. A lot of people, both keepers and guns, forget that dogs, like athletes, need training to become fit.

The Pointer Kennels were among the first, if not the first, to be registered by my Grandfather Hamilton at the Kennel Club when it was formed. When he was alive the kennel prefix was 'Brodick Castle' and Brodick Castle Sandy was a famous stud dog whose blood is in many of the Field Trial winners today. Fraser was a good dog handler, as were his assistants, John Anderson and George McAlpine, and together they took the pointers round the Field Trial circuit with enormous success and the dogs were exported all over the world.

When my father became Commissioner of my mother's Trust the prefix was changed to 'Isle of Arran' and in a very tiny way with a handful of dogs I am still trying to keep the flag flying with a little success myself. In 1981 my dog, 'Isle of Arran Larch' won the Pointer Breed Stake, The Champion Stake, and was second in the Postgraduate Dog Class at Crufts.

Pointers were not Mother's only interest. She kept Sealyhams, terriers which she showed, and was very keen on till she imported the first Schnauzer from Germany. Then she changed over completely to them and sold the Sealyhams. I never liked either one of those breeds as they both yapped and the Sealyhams had a habit of nipping my ankles as a child. Both Fraser and Mother knew so much about dogs and were so proud of them. Now when I read through the files of letters about the kennels I realise how awful was the disease of distemper which, on many occasions, nearly wiped out all the dogs. I see letters referring to twenty or even thirty dogs dying in one winter. There were no inoculations in those days, for no-one knew what the illness was. From the old letters I see my mother was convinced it was feeding, and would change the meal, or when others wrote to her of herbal cures she would try them. There was an isolation hospital built for the sick dogs and often Fraser would sit up all night nursing his beloved dogs, but with little success.

There can be little doubt that Arran must have ranked amongst the top sporting estates in the country. Not for big bags and driven shoots but for the active sportsman. Then, as now, about 150 stags were shot a year and 300 hinds. Quite often we are reported to have shot the heaviest stag in Scotland without any extra feeding in winter. This cull keeps the herd to a healthy number and we do not suffer from many winter deaths.

There are some sporting fishing burns. My father leased all but two to the Arran Angling Association. The grouse shooting used to be outstanding. About four days were driven, the rest was shooting over pointers. The average bag for each party would be 25 — 30 brace a day and the year's total for the island averaged about 6,000 brace. This lasted till the outbreak of war when the keepers left.

Every year there was a sale of gun dogs in London at Aldridges of St. Martin's Lane. I see from old catalogues that most years a draft of 30 or 40 young dogs was sent down to their sale.

In my childhood it was not just the number of birds shot nor the size of the head of the stag. No, it was a way of life. It built up to the Glorious 12th. Euston Station started to get busy the first week of August with people travelling to shooting lodges they had rented in the north of England and Scotland. Their household staff travelled with the household linen, the silver, food, wine and trunks of clothes. The keepers and their teams of dogs came with guns and rifles. Nearer the great day the shooting parties travelled with still more luggage. I was in Arran already and there was great excitement to go to the pier and meet the tenants I knew arriving off the boat. The Blains, travelling to the White House in Lamlash, which they did for 29 years, were like members of the family.

Old Mrs. Blain — Louisa — had a high-pitched screeching voice that could be heard from one end of the pier to the other. She called the dogs and her husband, Alfred, in one and the same voice and sentence, as they descended the gangway onto the pier. Mrs. Blain was a great character and was the first person I saw who did not dress in the ubiquitous tweeds, but instead used rather daring checked jersey suits. Round her waist an old Sam Brown belt with hooks on it from which she strung an old umbrella, a bottle of citronella for midges, an extra jersey, a waterproof, binoculars, to mention but a few things!

There came a time when my parents decided Dougarie Lodge was easier to let for the shooting season than the castle, so we stayed put and a long association started with the Russell family who took Dougarie for about twelve or

fourteen years. One of the family still comes back to the island to another shooting lodge in the north east of the island —Sannox House. So some of the old ties remain.

For several years Balfour Brown came to paint his series "The Life of a Stag" the prints of which are so expensive and sought after today. Fraser and he stalked the same stag each year and he grew into a fine beast and was, of course, sacrosanct.

One autumn we had a family who moved into Dougarie whom we, none of us, liked much. Fraser had driven Balfour Brown's stag away from the Dougarie boundary onto the Brodick ground, and kept a watchful eye on him. However, one Sunday the wife of the Dougarie tenant came to lunch at the castle and told my mother she had seen a magnificent stag near the road at the top of the hill. The next day, Monday, Fraser went to the pier in time for the early boat at 8.30 a.m. and there was his preciously guarded stag's head on the barrow. It could have only been the good lady herself who was to blame. Maybe we gave the dog a bad name, and hung it, but the same family had been known to shoot grouse on our side of the island, pack them in boxes, and post them off to their friends from Brodick Post Office.

The close friends of the family came year after year for shooting and stalking, and became friends of the keepers. It was an experience to go out into the beauty of a Scottish autumn with men well-versed in nature, and who knew every inch of their ground. They knew where the coveys of grouse were feeding, and if it was stalking they knew each beast intimately. The guests of the family enjoyed the company, the exercise, and the beauty and the artistry of stalking. It was indeed an art. A good stalker was expected to take you to within 70 yards of the beast you were to shoot, perhaps through a population of sheep or through the scattered members of a herd of deer without their becoming agitated or moving. A good clean shot through the neck was what was expected of the man firing the rifle, and if this was not accomplished in one shot it was the gentlemanly thing to do to hand your rifle to the stalker, who was usually an expert shot, so that the beast would be felled within a second.

My first stalk was in North Sannox Glen when I was quite

Grandmother "Tat", Angus and Mary

young and not very fit. Fraser and I had spied a bunch of stags half way up Suidh Ferguis and we set off to gain ground to get above these beasts. I was puffing and blowing in the

utmost discomfort. On we plodded and on we plodded, Fraser, as always, about 100 yards in front. I tried to draw his attention to the fact that we'd long passed the height where the herd of deer were, but he was too far ahead of me. Finally we reached the summit of Suidh Ferguis and, looking at my great discomfiture with the utmost disdain, he turned to me and said, with a sweep of his arm embracing the horizon,

"Yon's the finest view in Arran. I doubt you've ever seen it before and you'll never see it again," and with that he turned to go down the hill and stalk the deer. I have to admit he was right.

After a long crawl to get into the beasts ("keep your bottom down" is written on my heart) I became extremely nervous about the shot, and when I did shoot I had one clean miss after the other. It must have sounded like the Battle of Waterloo. The stags galloped off towards Sannox House and Fraser seized my rifle, saying,

"Ach, man, you'll never be like the others," meaning my brothers and sister whom he adored.

I got up from my knees feeling quite hopeless and at the same time extremely annoyed. I plodded off behind Fraser until he gave me a chance of a second shot. So angry was I that with no nerve I not only shot the stag that was pointed out to me, but the neighbour as well, a left and a right. Again this didn't please him, because you were only supposed to shoot the one particular stag he selected. Not only did I have his annoyance to face but when I got home the annoyance of my mother as well.

14

BROTHERS AND SISTER

OOKING back, it is my brother Angus, now 7th Duke of Montrose, that I remember most in my childhood. It was Angus who taught me how to read the time on the clock. It was he who cut a large circle of white cardboard with the figures on the clock represented by birds, mice, beetles, dogs and cats. It was Angus who kept jackdaws and ravens in two cages on the battlement of Brodick Castle. And it was he who took me for walks up into the hills and, when I could walk no further, gave me piggybacks to the top of the hills overlooking Glen Rosa and onto the shoulder of Goatfell. Even in those days I was no lightweight, but he was tremendously strong.

At the time we went for these walks I did not appreciate what an outstanding young man was taking time to spend with his kid sister. He was in Pop at Eton and also Keeper of the Oppidan's Wall. He boxed well and rowed well, he shot well and was very, very good-looking.

When Angus, Mary and Ronald were all home, plus their friends, the house came alive. They had a wonderful time, but, being so much older than I, they were out most of the day shooting, or lobster potting in our motor boat *THE CRUBAN* or trying to aquaplane on a board behind the boat. However, she was so slow it was impossible to keep standing on the board for long. Nevertheless a lot of fun was had by all.

For the whole of one holiday Angus sat at the piano, having first stuck a piece of paper with the letter denoting each note on the keyboard, hitting one note over and over again till he sang it in tune, then singing doh-ray-me. He went on practising till we felt like throwing something at him, but he ended up good enough to compete in the Gaelic Mod and won sufficient points to get 3rd place in the Gold Medal Competition.

Having taken his degree Angus got a job with A.E. & I. Agricultural Department and was sent to Rhodesia to help with the problem of soil erosion. Before going, in October 1930 he married Isobel Sellar and they had one of the biggest weddings of the Season.

Preparing for the great day of the wedding, Father, having looked in the mirror, discovered that the middle-aged spread had caught up with him. Evidently he had read in some paper that there was a firm by the name of Spirella which aided those who were suffering from the same spread. The advertisement probably mentioned that corsets were available for men as well as for women. Without thinking too carefully that there might be two different shops at which two different sexes bought their supports, he went into the nearest shop by the name of Spirella, in Edinburgh.

The sales lady was highly surprised to see this man coming in and, knowing Father's loud voice, she must have been fairly embarrassed as well. It may have dawned on him that he was in the wrong department but he, too, became embarrassed and said,

"I have come for one of your er ..... garments ..... on ..... well, for my daughter, you understand. She's a little like — ", and he patted his hands round his middle, "like that."

The lady said she quite understood, probably thinking that the daughter was pregnant, and asked what size his daughter was.

"Oh well," he said, "let me think, well, I suppose she is probably just about my size," still tapping his tummy.

144

Angus and his bride, Isobel Sellar

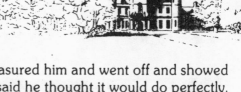

And so the lady measured him and went off and showed him the garment. He said he thought it would do perfectly. She packed it up and he went off down the street clutching his parcel.

When he came to dress for the wedding the valet, Bobby, had his kilt, plaid, and all the accoutrements laid out on the bed, and then Father produced this garment. The valet, of course, had never seen such a thing before, and neither had Father, so between them my father struggled into the stays which had long laces attached. Father tried to pull the laces tight and then handed them to Bobby.

"Go on, Bobby! Pull! Pull harder and tighter!" he shouted.

Eventually he was strapped in and the laces were tied. By this time it was getting late and the car had arrived to take my mother and father to St. Giles Cathedral, so he quickly strapped on his kilt, sporran, jacket and plaid and was just leaving his room to go down the stairs when Bobby clutched him by the hand in fits of laughter, seeing that the kilt was fast slipping down past his knees. My father was in a hurry and cried,

"Go on, leave me alone! Leave me alone!"

But Bobby persisted and grabbed him by the arm and showed him his kilt which by this time was down around the calves of his legs. He had to go back to his room and take the Spirella stays off. By this time there was no hope of trying to fit it on in any other way, so he had to go to St. Giles with the middle-aged spread as it normally was!

For the wedding Angus was dressed in the full Highland regalia of a chieftain's son — golden eagle feathers in his bonnet, green velvet doublet, lace jabot, Graham tartan kilt and plaid fastened by a silver plaid brooch with a large Cairngorm mounted in it. He looked magnificent, standing 6'4" tall. Isobel was just 5'4" and dressed with a beautiful lace veil over a satin dress, looking very delicate beside him.

Special trains were run from Arran for the tenants and the employees, and a meal was provided for the guests before the wedding. The Buchanan contingent came by bus. There was a big reception in Heriot Row and then the bride and bridegroom left for an unknown destination.

In fact, they drove down to Ardrossan and got on the same boat as the Arran wedding guests, sailing into Brodick Bay in time to see a bonfire in the field near the castle where there was plenty of refreshment and dancing round the fire, all of which they joined in before driving to Dougarie Lodge for their honeymoon.

On February 21st, 1931 they sailed for Rhodesia to take up his appointment as the A.E. & I. Field Officer. They stayed at the Windsor Hotel in Salisbury which, at that time was quite a small town. Another young man going for the first time to Rhodesia who travelled with them, was Humphrey Gibbs. He, too, made his home there, and it was a great sorrow to Angus that in the 1970s they found themselves in opposite political camps.

Angus lived and worked from Salisbury for some years. Soon after his first baby, Fiona, was born, and not long before A.E. & I. were going to post him to Canada, my grandmother took a winter's cruise out to South Africa and up to Rhodesia to visit him. There she found that he had entirely fallen in love with the country and its people, the casual life, the wild, undeveloped hugeness of the place. Without referring to Mother or Father, she gave him £2,000, and with £1,000 from the Rhodesian government he bought his first farm.

This was her last serious influence on the family, but with what far-reaching results.

Mother and Father were furious with her, Father particularly,

as he felt his son should return home and take his place in this country.

Angus bought ground 90 miles from Salisbury to the north, just wild bush land from which he had to cut out his land, clear it and then start farming it, ploughing it with spans of oxen.

My brother Ronald, having spent a year serving in the R.N.V.R., went to Cambridge and then he, too, decided he would try his luck in Africa. Public opinion has changed so much that it is hard to remember that it was considered a great service to the Empire for young men to go from the United Kingdom to the totally undeveloped countries and try to help develop them.

He went to Que Que near Bulawayo and found a job opening up a gold mine. While there he got the sack from his job. The people he was working for were a tough bunch. An African got badly hurt in an accident and the Manager was not going to send him to hospital because he wanted no inspections and no questions on his safety arrangements at the mine. Ronald wouldn't stand for that and put the wounded African into his car and drove him to a hospital in Bulawayo. When he returned to the mine he found he was jobless.

How typical of Ronald, the gentle one, he was the least flamboyant of us all, gentle and kind, he always had time to listen to people, which is what the world needs so badly. Young and old, rich and poor were all the same to Ronald, he always had time for them. He shared a sense of the ridiculous and enjoyed meeting people and was always full of life. He was the only baby born in Brodick Castle in hundreds of years and was known locally as "The Arran Boy".

In the Spring of 1931 my sister married John Boscawen. Even at that young age he was an extremely knowledgeable

The wedding of my sister and John Boscawen

gardener. He was a cousin of the Dorrien-Smiths who own the Scilly Isles and the world famous garden of Tresco. During the First World War he had been evacuated there, and Major Arthur Dorrien-Smith had given all his young nephews, and his own family, jobs to do. John Boscawen had been put into the garden to work, which created a lifelong interest he shared with his own parents who had a beautiful garden.

He married Mary in St. Martins-in-the-Field, London, which was filled with friends and people brought from Arran and Buchanan. She was to have been married by Cosmo Gordon Lang, Archbishop of Canterbury, but unfortunately illness prevented him from attending the wedding.

On the day, Mother went ahead to the church and left

Father to bring Mary: but Mary and he had a hilarious luncheon and, having set off in great form, they were half-way to St. Martins when Mary suddenly realized she had forgotten to put on her veil. They had to turn the car and go back to the house, by which time there was no maid left there and Father tried to pin the veil on, but, of course, the more he tried the more he laughed, and the more impossible the situation became. They didn't have time to be too particular, but somehow anchored it down and set off again. By this time they were both shaking with nerves at being so late and instead of the leisurely pace up the aisle as they had planned, they raced up, taking one verse of the hymn to reach the altar!

Each summer John and Mary came to Brodick for their holidays and, evening after evening, after being out shooting, Mary would be left as a "gardening widow" while John went off with Mother. Together they laid out Brodick Castle gardens, which now belong to the National Trust, and which are probably second to none in Scotland.

The type of soil we have dictated a collection of rhododendrons, and John knew so many people in the gardening world that it was not long before acres and acres of rhododendron and camelia developed, and large beds of lilies and exotic plants.

Major Arthur Dorrien-Smith sent up a puffer (a shallow draughted coastal vessel) with plants from the Scilly Isles. John introduced Mother to Kingdon Ward, one famed for his expeditions to Indo China where he collected rhododendrons, and arranged for him to stay at Brodick. We used to tease them considerably because while great economies were being effected in many directions, each summer another acre of woodland garden would be taken in hand.

The expeditions to Nepal and Indo China were financed

by people, as well as Societies, taking shares, then on their return to Britain the plants and seeds were divided among the shareholders in proportion to the money they had given. Hampers of plants arrived at Brodick, each plant and seed packet numbered. When they grew and flowered the Botanic Gardens were notified and an expert arrived to name a new plant or discard one already classified. John Boscawen was good at striking cuttings so Kingdon Ward gave him extra plants to deal with.

John and Mary were a very lucky couple because when they married they had to live in London, as my brother-in-law worked on the Stock Exchange. They were not very flush for money and an eccentric aunt, Lady Whitnam, sent for my sister to come and see her in her London house where she had been bedridden for about 20 years. It was always a question as to whether it was necessary for her to be bedridden; but she had taken offence at one of her husband's operatic girlfriends and had retired to bed where, dressed in a black velvet bed jacket with a white lace collar, she had remained, whilst still keeping on a large house in the country and a chauffeur and car. She summoned those she wanted to see, and if any doctor suggested she was not ill she sacked the doctor. Strangely enough, after all these years in bed, her leg muscles had not shrivelled at all. The doctors were sure she got up and exercised at night!

She sent for Mary and demanded a plan of the house she was to live in, in Onslow Square. She then had furniture, which she listed, brought up from the country house carried up to her bedroom, measured in front of her, and fitted into the plan of the house, by this method furnishing most of the rooms. The trouble was that there had been a mismeasurement, and had a bed that she had placed against a particular wall been left *in situ* it would have been only a few inches from an

electric fire. My sister had moved that, and quite a lot of the furniture around the house, to please herself.

One afternoon there was a tap on the door and Lady Whitnam's maid was on the doorstep, plan in hand, because the old lady wished to know if the furniture was in the correct position. However, a cup of tea and a friendly chat was sufficient for the maid to return and say the house looked beautiful, and all was in its correct position!

15

SHARED SPORT AT BUCHANAN

OON after Angus left for Rhodesia his great friend John M. Bannerman arrived at Buchanan and took up his position as Farm Manager, later to become factor at Buchanan, making use of his Agricultural degree. For the first winter he lived in a room in Buchanan Castle and became more like a brother to me and was extremely good with children.

As a character he had great charisma and vitalised any gathering he was amongst. He soon got my mother interested in the subject of Gaelic and Gaelic music. At weekends some of his Gaelic friends came down to Buchanan and we had ceilidhs so that Gaelic music became part of my young life.

John was still playing a certain amount of rugger and would very often take me with him to watch matches in Glasgow, and always arranged for us all to have tickets for the international matches at Murrayfield.

In 1931 he married Ray Mundel, whose home had been near Lairg, and they moved into the factor's house, the Old Manse at Balmaha, where they raised their family of four children.

Some winter evenings John and I would go duck flighting on the Low Mains of Buchanan, long rough, reedy pastures beside the River Endrick, marshy, windswept, wild places. In the distance the islands in Loch Lomond stood dark against the wintery sky; but the Low Mains were not much higher than the river bank and the tall reeds hid the loch itself. Only the rounded tree-clad tops of the islands showed dark beyond the reeds of burnished gold.

The area was interspersed with deep, wide, dutch-like dykes, the widest of all being the Croman Ditch. He could only drive his Hillman Minx as far as the burn at the High Mains. There we gathered together cartridges and game bags and donned our gum boots, scarves and any other warming clothes we had — oilskins, woollen sweaters and tweeds. His cocker spaniel was keen to get started.

The frost was crisp under our feet and we slipped and slithered over the ground poached by the cattle. Ice would give way and we would sink into the muddy holes. The stubble field, the *Curragh Glas* sheltered from the wind by tall old oaks and a jungle of alders and birch led us down to the gate which we passed through between the two woods to the riverside. We turned right over an arched stone bridge spanning one of the dykes and took up our position near an old willow tree split by lightning long ago. The expanse of wildness was large about us and the cry of wader birds rang out in the winter's evening. Dark clouds rose above the hills on the far side of Loch Lomond, the hills beside Luss and Tarbert, but the sun set further to our left beyond where the industrial town of Balloch lay. Only the edges of the clouds caught the red fire of the sun long since set from terrestrial eyes.

The duck egg blue of a winter sky changed to gold and the palest cream as it touched the horizon. We could hear geese calling on the loch ready for flight up into the stubble field, or with any luck, the freshwater pond that lay in front us. It was bitter cold and for some long time nothing happened except the odd plop of a water rat or vole as it entered the river, or perhaps a pike jumped. And then there was a swirl of wings overhead as some mallard passed out of shot along the line of the river. Unseen and in a flash a wigeon landed in the

154

Mr and Mrs John Bannerman, later the Liberal Peer Baron Bannerman of Kildonan OBE

pool in front of us, and John might get one shot before it took flight again.

It was only on the worst possible nights of storm and gale with lashing rain and hail that the geese flew low enough to really give some shooting, and then we might be lucky to get four or five before we trudged back by torchlight to the car.

If Father came out he would have to make his stand at the nearest point to the transport because with his type of deafness he lost his balance in the dark. I would help him home by carrying his gun and walking arm in arm. He was a big man and when he lurched badly I often had difficulty in holding him.

Years later I learned that we were not the only people to enjoy the sport of the Low Mains. When the European War was nearing an end I went as a Red Cross Welfare Officer out to India, sailing on a troopship from Liverpool. I was stationed at a hospital in Poona at the time when the prisoners of war were returning from the Japanese prison camps. A new batch of men arrived at the hospital and the Red Cross Welfare Officer's job was to go round and take their names and numbers, the units from which they had been captured, and to offer them a Red Cross letter and telegram to be sent to their next of kin free of charge.

In this new batch was a large dark man, Stoker Kerr, one of the few who survived the tragedy of the sinking of *H.M.S. Repulse.* He was polite enough. He gave me his name and his address, which was the Vale of Leven, near Balloch by Loch Lomondside. I offered him the Red Cross letter but he said "No". I offered him the Red Cross cable form and he said "No". It crossed my mind he might be illiterate. I offered him books, he said "No". I offered to do his shopping, he said "No". I left the man in peace, sitting at the end of his bed gazing at the floor in silence.

This went on for several days, Stoker Kerr was always sitting at the end of his bed staring at the floor. He never spoke to any of the other men or any of the nursing staff. The Ward Sister called me into her office one day and told me I must do something about Stoker Kerr or he'd go off his rocker. I told her I was feeling extremely ill at that moment and was going to the Sick Bay but I'd pass her message on to which ever girl was to take my place. I had dysentery for the third time since I had been in India and was put into the Sick Sister's ward within the same compound as the hospital.

They were long, low buildings with a door opening onto a verandah to give shade from the blazing sun striking the red sand and the rocks between the wards, about 20 yards apart. I was lying there one day reading quietly when I heard someone walking along the verandah on crutches. Suddenly the whole of my doorway was filled with the large frame of Stoker Kerr. I said,

"How nice of you to come and see me," a remark which was met with silence.

He propped his crutches up against the wall and took a seat in the chair, easing his trouser legs comfortably over his knees, and fixed me with a glare as he said,

"I'm no very good with the women, the mother died, the faither married again and we didnae like the woman so we turned the faither out back at the Vale." (Vale of Leven).

I said, "Oh, who keeps house for you?"

"The sister. And she married a foreigner and he wore glasses, of course."

"Really! There were a lot of Poles stationed in that area at the beginning of the war."

"No," said Stoker Kerr, "he wasnae a Pole, he was an Englishman."

End of conversation.

I wasn't sure if he knew who I was but I felt I had nothing to lose by telling him from where I came. The chief thing was to keep him talking after the ward sister's warning that he would go bonkers if he didn't talk. And so I said,

"You know I come from quite near your home, I come from Buchanan Castle just across the loch from Balloch".

It was like unlocking a long locked door. A smile came on his face.

"Buchanan!" he said, with all the feeling of excitement of a happy memory of long ago. "Buchanan!" he repeated. "Oh, mony's the nicht the brother and I and the long dogs had at Buchanan." He pulled his chair up against my bed and talked of nights of poaching. Taking matches one by one from his box he laid them on the bedcover, explaining,

"This is the way we came. We kept close to the islands, there, in the shadows on a moonlicht nicht," placing another match to represent Inchmurrin, "running the outboard engine, then to the shadows of Creinch along to Inchcaillach, then we turned the engine off, it was too close to Balmaha and we might have been heard in the village there (another match) then we rowed silently into the river mouth." And then he described ditch by ditch and dyke by dyke where the brother got out of the boat with his long dogs (greyhounds) and here they set their rabbit nets against the dyke and they eased their boat up the Croman Ditch and drove the rabbits into the nets. Back into the boat again and higher up the river, up to the old willow tree split by lightning with the pool beside it.

"That was the place," he said, "that was the place." He laid out the map of the whole area with matches. "There's an old stone bridge there, and then the hedge, that the rabbits burrow beneath. It leads up to an oak wood with all the rough trees below them. That's where the pheasants roost. We used to take long poles with wire snares at the end and you could pluck them off the branches of those trees like grapes off a vine. That was a great place there. Your keepers nearly caught us one day, they were lying in wait for us, the buggers, up by the wood where the dogs were. There was one hidden by the old stone bridge and another by the willow tree. They let my brother set the nets and just chasing the rabbits into the nets when they came at him from every direction. He had just about made the boat when yon big tall hulk of a man you had tackled him and they both went in the river and they both just missed the boat. I scarpered then and called the dogs to me lower down the river. They got the brother but it was an awful daft thing to do."

"That wasn't a keeper, that was my brother Ronald." I said.

He chuckled and said, "Maybe, but it was daft all the same."

I said, "Well, it didn't do your brother any harm. They took him back to the stables and locked him up then they all had a cup of tea and waited for the police to come. As far as I know when the police did come they all sat around discussing poaching, and in the end your brother got off and walked back to Balloch".

We discussed the whole area in detail until my tea arrived and he had to back to the ward. He got up and collected his crutches and stood looking at me from the doorway, and said,

"Just the same he *was* daft, awfu' daft."

I wonder if the next generation of Kerrs still manage to have their sport, and if they think the ecologists working in Inchcaillach known locally as "the beetle boys" are "Daft, awfu' daft", or whether the Nature Conservancy, who now have an interest in the area, have managed to stop them navigating the River Endrick where our keepers failed. I

don't know because I don't live there any more, but I wouldn't mind taking a bet!

16

VISIT TO AFRICA

N the winter of 1931 when I was twelve, I started having pains in my left hand which was immediately X-rayed, and once again, osteomyelitis was discovered. It was the worst possible time for a girl to be at a disadvantage and to have her hand in plaster and her arm in a sling. I began to hate going round with the other young people. I disliked the fact that they could play tennis and games and seemed so full of life. But for me, the regime started again of early bed and resting in the afternoon, X-rays and doctors' appointments in Glasgow. I became very shut off. My father said, one day,

"Come on, old girl, we'll go for a walk," and he and I set off, arm in arm.

He talked to me seriously about how lucky I was to have two arms and two legs and to be mentally sane. He told me about the young deaf people he had so much to do with as Chairman of the Deaf Institute. He told me of crippled children who had learnt to write by holding their pen or paintbrush in their teeth or, in some instances, in their toes, and how they could write and paint pictures in this way. Later he showed me photographs of the pictures they had done.

"Now then," he announced, "this afternoon we will play tennis."

And though I swore I couldn't do it, he insisted.

He was not satisfied that I tried to lift the ball on my tennis racquet and serve underhand. I had to flick the ball onto my

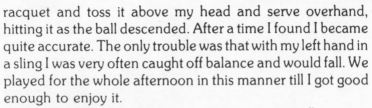

racquet and toss it above my head and serve overhand, hitting it as the ball descended. After a time I found I became quite accurate. The only trouble was that with my left hand in a sling I was very often caught off balance and would fall. We played for the whole afternoon in this manner till I got good enough to enjoy it.

Next day he said, "Now we are going to swim."

And, dear soul, dressed in his woollen bathing suit belonging to a previous generation, of pale blue, dark blue and white horizontal stripes with elbow length sleeves and shorts that came down to his thighs, we went down to the shore below the castle.

"I'll race you," he said, "by swimming with my right hand only and you keep your plaster out of the water. As you can't manage to do the breaststroke you'll have to lie on your back and paddle with one hand and swim like mad with your feet, swinging your right hand only."

In this manner we swam quite a length of Brodick Bay and had fun doing it. After that we dried and changed, and I was made to try to play golf with the right hand only, which was not so easy. But at least I managed the short shots and the putting.

Having given me his great care and attention, I was once more thrown amongst young people and found that I could join in with them, and that really they didn't pay any attention to my extreme awkwardness. I managed to integrate perfectly well.

The only bore was having to rest so much. However, for the winter months of 1932 it was decided it would be better for me to get out of the cold, damp climate of Scotland, and my governess, who at this time was Miss Elliott, and I were sent to St. Austell's Bay Hotel in Devon. There we did lessons and lived a peaceful, quiet existence with a lot of rest.

Myself aged fifteen

We travelled round a little, and before long moved on down to St. Ives, and then a short visit to Tresco Island to stay with the Dorrien-Smiths. Miss Elliott and I stayed for some weeks at Tresco Abbey and a more lovely place I can't imagine, surrounded by superb gardens, the acres of small farms growing daffodils, the miles of silver sand and turquoise blue sea which raced across them as the tide came in.

After a month or two when Father and Mother could get away from home, they picked me up to go to Rhodesia to stay with my brother Angus. They met me in London, with Bobby the valet and Christina the maid, and we joined the Union Castle liner *Caernarvon Castle*, which was one of the finest ships in the Union Castle fleet in those days.

About the second day out we discovered that a few cabins away from ours was the Chapman family. Stuart Chapman had been in the next room to me in the Tuberculin Sanitorium in Leysin when we were both three years old. Stuart was desperately ill at this time, but so cheerful, and it was nice to

RMMV Caernarvon Castle at Madeira

164

see him again. We spent many long hours on deck reminiscing about our days in Switzerland. I was lucky, I came back from Africa. He didn't.

Also on board was Sir Abe Baillie, the great financier, and a gathering of well-known people of the day, so my father enjoyed his tour talking politics, and my mother enjoyed the relaxation of having nothing to do for a few weeks and I, of course, loved the deck games and the swimming pool.

The first two weeks in Africa we spent at a house inland from Cape Town at the village of Montague, which is on the edge of the Little Karoo Desert. Mother and I spent a lot of time painting the wild flowers of the place or going for walks along the foothills listening to the baboons chattering in the rocks above us, and bathing in the hot sulphur springs. I am told that now it has developed into quite a health resort, but in those days there was nothing there but Mrs.Slesinger's house and a few Dutch farmers' houses, and the sulphur springs were in a simple thatched wooden shelter.

From a station which was a whole day's drive across the desert, we took the train up to Salisbury which was an undeveloped town of just a few thousand white people. The streets, made wide enough to turn a span of 16 oxen, were just beginning to be tarmacced. Avenues of jacaranda trees planted down each side of one street, flame trees down another and frangipanni in another. The houses and shops were mostly on the old Colonial design of concrete floors to protect them against the ravages of white ants, and the superstructure of wood with wide verandahs surrounded by mosquito netting.

Salisbury stands on a plateau about four thousand feet above sea level and has a wonderful climate. To see it now, only fifty years later, is staggering. A fine modern town of skyscrapers, modern shops, public gardens, sports clubs and

Angus's car on the way to Banket, our first day. Christina fixing fifty sacks on its bumper

streets full of traffic.

My brother and my sister-in-law met us with their children and we stayed a night or two in town. Then we set off for his farm. I went with Angus and the luggage in one car, and my mother and father went with my sister-in-law, Isobel, Bobby the valet, and the maid in another.

The tarmac road was only in the town and went no distance at all out of Salisbury. There were tar strips or tar mats which were laid just the width of the car's wheels and if you skidded or slipped off these in the dry season you put up a cloud of red dust and were lucky if you didn't split your tyres. In the wet season you almost certainly skidded into the wide monsoon ditches.

We drove on, getting hotter and dustier, till the tarmac finished and the dust road began. Many miles on again we branched off the dust road across the veldt with grass so high that it was above the bonnet of the car.

We followed the line of rail in a northerly direction to the train halt of Banket. The tar strips stretched about 14 miles from Salisbury, but my brother's farm was 90 miles out of town, far beyond Banket, then a right turn into the bush.

We bashed through the grass and bumped and swung for the rest of the day until we came to his steading. The nearest white couple were 30 miles away.

For two years Angus and his wife, with a Gaelic-speaking Nanny and their children, Fiona and Seumas, had lived in rondavels or round mud huts with thatched roofs built on a rocky hill crest or *kopje.* Just before we arrived there had nearly been an accident, for when my sister-in-law looked out of the window she saw several baboons chattering and nattering around Fiona's pram, about to take her away with them. Isobel yelled and screamed at the baboons and shouted for help from the Africans to drive the baboons away, which luckily they did.

For some weeks my brother had been making bricks and baking them to build a house in honour of our coming, and a very fine house it was. The only thing they had had no time to do was the plumbing, neither had they much furniture. The dressing table was made of tea boxes laid on their sides and covered in cotton drapes where Mother and I, who shared a room, could put our clothes. Father and the valet were sent up to the rondavels, half a mile away, to sleep, and the children had their own nursery near Angus and Isobel.

About the second night there the cat produced kittens in my underclothes. I need hardly describe the mess that this caused. Then about the fourth night we were there the guard dog set upon (in the sitting room!) one of the local mongrels that came scrounging round the dustbins. I have never heard such noise and such screams. I was so horrified I was almost

sick. In the end the poor dog had to have its throat cut it was so badly hurt and I was a jittering wreck of nerves.

That was by no means the end of the horrors because a few days later, when driving round the farm, my brother and I came upon some Africans trying to kill a bullock by throwing machetes at it, and this poor, wretched, bleeding, wounded animal was still gallantly trying to gallop from them. I decided at that moment that I was not tough enough to stand the colonial life. Little did I know that I was going to have to after I had married. However, all was not so traumatic and we had a happy stay.

Father and Bobby the valet certainly seemed to enjoy themselves trying to do the plumbing, arguing amongst themselves like a couple of old cronies. One thing they completely forgot was the heat of the African sun. They put the water tank on the roof in full sunlight which meant that by day, if you wanted hot water, you turned on the cold tap, and by night when the stove was lit, you turned on the hot tap. I don't know if anybody ever put this right, but we left it like that.

My mother, as usual, being keen on farming, found my brother's life extremely interesting. He had done an immense amount of work breaking in virgin soil straight from the bush into rich, cultivated farmland. In fact, with my brother's knowledge of agriculture, his crops, mostly tobacco, though some maize, were extremely good.

While we were there we heard on the radio that King George V had died, so we returned to Salisbury and were there in time for a memorial service for His Majesty in the lovely whitewashed Church of Scotland in the centre of the town.

We took a train from Salisbury and went up to see the Victoria Falls, staying in the hotel which was very basic in

those days. Like an idiot, I dived into the swimming pool, hitting the bottom and broke my nose, which caused endless trouble later on.

We had a wonderful time being shown round by the curator of the Nature Reserve at Livingstone and climbed right down to the foot of the falls which is known as "The Boiling Pot" and went for walks along the Rain Forest where the spray from the falls produced so much water it is like being out in pouring rain. It was all so peaceful and the natives so friendly, one thought nothing of wandering around the bush on one's own. From Livingstone we went back into Salisbury, down to Bulawayo to visit Rhodes's grave on the Motopos Hills.

We were driven out of Bulawayo by a mutual friend of Father's and Rhodes's and left the car at the foot of the rocky hill, a huge solid rock of some hundred or more feet with boulders strewn about on its surface. From the top of the hill one can see mile upon mile of African bush dotted with green acres of farms. The two men stood reminiscing of the days of the Boer War, of weekends staying at Groote Schur, Rhodes's elegant large white house built on the lines of a Dutch farm-house, with their characteristic gables. It was situated near Cape Town and became the home of the Prime Minister of South Africa latterly.

Father was a great admirer of Rhodes and in width of vision must have been very like him. He listened to his talk of a railway and a road going straight from Cape to Cairo, of his advice to the young — "Go North, young man, go North" — always on and on to open up the continent. At Groote Schur they met and had long evenings of conversation with people of interest. At one dinner party Sir David Gill, the Astronomer Royal at the Cape, with a lovely Aberdonian brogue, was telling how many threepenny pieces it would take, when put all in line to reach from the earth to the sun. Rudyard Kipling, the other guest, chipped in: "Even without your brogue, David, I would know what country you came from; no-one else in the world but a Scot would bother his head to count how many three-penny bits it takes to reach the sun!"

We went on down to Johannesburg where we met Samuel Alexander, well-known in the diamond trade, and who was called Uncle Sam by all who knew him. There is a story of a taxi driver in

Gracie Fields and Father

Johannesburg who was tipped rather meanly by Uncle Sam, so the taxi driver drew his attention to the fact, saying,

"When I drive your son he gives me twice as much as that."

"Of course," said Uncle Sam, "but there's one great difference. He has a rich father!"

In his company we met Gracie Fields, who was doing a tour of the area, and she couldn't have been sweeter to me. One of my most favourite possessions is a beaded African belt that she gave me, though unfortunately it no longer fits

me! Later she came home on the same ship as we did, *The Stirling Castle*, with her brother, Tommy Fields.

We left via Pretoria and reached Durban, resting a while after days in the train, then took a Union Castle liner to Port Elisabeth from where we hired a car and drove down what is known as the Garden Route to Cape Town, passing on the way teams of fourteen donkeys pulling loads, and spans of oxen. The road was dirt track most of that long distance, and very rough indeed.

We ended up staying at Muizenberg where I had the most wonderful time bathing and learning to surf ride. I went with my parents to visit friends of theirs in Simonstown, the naval base, and Wynberg to various fruit farms.

We visited an ostrich farm and watched them cutting the feathers which, at that time, were highly prized for capes and decorating ladies' hats. I was given a fan of huge pink feathers by Sir Abe Baillie which I used when I was presented at Court in 1939. Ostrich feather evening capes and boas were the height of fashion and most of the large Ascot hats had feathers on them or were made entirely of feathers. The ostriches were somehow manhandled, blindfolded, and then driven into a small triangular trap which just fitted them so that they could have their feathers cut. Now, one never sees an ostrich feather so I suppose those farms are closed or perhaps carry on solely for the ostrich meat so dear to the Dutch for making their *biltong* — dried strips of ostrich meat.

We were not long home in Scotland when we heard Angus's little daughter Fiona had been taken ill with appendicitis. By then the rains had come and Angus and Isobel had to drive 90 miles into Salisbury with this critically ill child, aged about 4, through the jungle of grass I have just described, and over the rivers, which by now were fairly

Ostriches in the mud compound before being clipped

high before they got to Salisbury. Her appendix was burst for seven hours before she was operated on by Dr. Bert Honey.

While out in Rhodesia it became evident that Angus's marriage was not a happy one, and with their devout religious beliefs divorce was anathema to Mother and Father. When we arrived back in London from Rhodesia we found Ronald waiting to meet them to tell them that he intended to marry Nancy Ryder whose marriage had also broken and who already had five children. The blow was incredibly hard for them.

These two blows coming as they did, one on top of the other, were instrumental, I think, in Ronald getting a harder deal than he would otherwise have done. They disinherited him and cut him off, and I did not see him until the war when, largely through my father's sister, Aunt Helen, pleading, they invited Ronald and Nancy to stay in Arran. By the time my own marriage broke they had softened considerably. In fact, Ronald's was the happiest marriage you could imagine, and for 40 years until his death Ronald and Nancy were inseparable. He never had any children of his own.

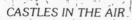

17

SHADOWS OF THE FUTURE

 Y parents decided in 1932 that they would have to move out of Buchanan Castle. After much consideration they decided to alter one of the farmhouses on the estate, Auchmar, nearer to Loch Lomond, with an uninterrupted view of the loch over sloping green fields with the Conic hill giving shelter from the north wind and the music of a burn running through the garden below the bedroom windows.

Father did what he could with his old home. He thought he was doing the right thing and rather daringly he made it into a hotel. Instead of going wholeheartedly into the business and joining a chain or a company or even getting professional managers, he got a very dear cousin of my mother's, Patrick Acheson and his wife Norah, to come and run it. They had a very limited knowledge of the business, but even so, they soon realised that Father was on the wrong track. The first year was not so bad because he managed to get the whole summer leased to the Cunard Shipping Company for their rich American tourists so everyone knew where they stood. The following year he *would* have everything run as for a large country house, with vast and extravagant menus of salmon and venison and grouse, no public bars were anticipated, there was no question of opening the reception rooms for Glasgow functions, there was no question of dividing the large bedrooms or conserving heat or any short cuts to economy. He struggled on until 1939.

Auchmar seemed extraordinarily small at the time and only their most treasured possessions were moved in. Now

Auchmar 1935

my nephew, his wife and three children live there. They have managed to let two flats without feeling cramped at all, such is the change of outlook today.

The addition to Auchmar was finished in the autumn of 1932. Simultaneously we heard that my Hamilton grandmother had terminal cancer. She was living at Auchrannie in Brodick so Mother spent most of that autumn dashing between Brodick and Auchmar.

She died in 1934 and Mother was distraught with sorrow after her lifelong companionship. It was a miserable winter, cold and grey and foggy and there was really nothing to cheer Mother up. Father came to me one day and said,

"What your mother wants is a good holiday to get away from it all and have a nice rest. I know just the place for her to go. There's a fellow who plays the fiddle at Eastbourne," (this, it transpired, was Albert Sandler with the Palm Court

Orchestra at the Grand Hotel). He continued, "Now, we'll do the whole thing in comfort. You and she and her lady's maid and Tommy Watson, the chauffeur, will drive down there and break the journey in the Lake District. I will follow on with the luggage as I have some meetings to attend in Edinburgh and in London. You must persuade her to go."

But every time I spoke to Mother about it she dissolved into tears and assured me that she only wanted to rest in her lovely, comfortable new home, with her own things around her, her fire and her dogs. However, we both knew that when Father made up his mind to do something it was no good arguing. And so when the day of departure came the chauffeur took a case for each of us and left it with the hall porter at the Central Hotel, Glasgow, where my father, travelling from Brodick, would pick them up. My case was marked with the initials 'JG' and Mother's 'MM', her lady's maid had a label with 'Christina Munn' on it, and the chauffeur a label with 'Tommy Watson', and we four set off in the car which was freezing cold, down to the Lake District.

There were icy roads, making the driving conditions bad. We arrived late at the hotel in the Lake District. I doubt if there was any heating at all, certainly the place was damp and our little party was an extremely miserable one. However, we continued on the next day to Eastbourne where Father should have joined us soon after tea.

He, meanwhile, had picked up our cases in Glasgow, continued to Edinburgh and left them all in the left luggage office where they were stamped with a pink ticket. He went to the R.N.L.I. meeting of which he was Chairman for Scotland, had dinner, then called for a porter to put the luggage on the London train. I have no doubt that the porter told him where he put all the luggage, but Father would not have heard him. So when he got to Euston and called another porter he told

him that there were five suitcases which included his own, in the Guard's Van, all with the pink stamp of the Edinburgh Left Luggage Office on them. These he took and placed in the Euston Left Luggage while he went to the Euston Hotel for a bath and a shave and breakfast, signing himself "James Graham, Auchmar, Drymen" because he thought he could tip less, though I am sure that the staff at Euston knew him perfectly well because he had used the hotel all his life. He then went to the House of Lords and attended meetings there. He came back to Euston by taxi to collect the luggage and transfer it across London to catch the train to Eastbourne.

One of Father's foibles was that he couldn't bear anybody touching his shoulder or his arm — he immediately thought they were drunk. Many a time he has said to me,

"I met that friend of yours in Glasgow, must have been drunk, he caught me by the arm".

No matter how much I said that the man was a tee-totaller he was not convinced. So when he got to the Left Luggage Office and two men came up, one on each side of him, and touched him on the shoulders, in his excessively loud voice that deaf people so often have, he started shouting,

"Get away! Get out! Go away, leave me alone!" waving his umbrella to drive the men off. He was much astonished when they bent his arms behind his back and lifted him by the trouser seat and frog-marched him off to a Black Maria!

Meanwhile Mother and I had settled into our hotel and had tea and waited and waited. We had dinner, we still waited. As usual she was convinced that he had lost his balance and fallen in front of a car or that there had been some other accident. In her nervous state she worked herself into a panic. I was sent up to bed but she waited on downstairs. Then at about half past ten at night my bedroom door flew open and Mother rushed in and threw herself across the foot of my bed, and through a flood of tears said,

"They've got your father!"

I sat bolt upright and said, "Who's got my father?"

"The police!" she said, which was the most stunning statement at that time of night. "They've arrested him for disturbance of the peace, resisting arrest and stealing a suitcase, it's so unlike him!"

I comforted her the best way I could and saw her into her room to bed. It wasn't until the next morning that I heard the full story, when Father arrived off the milk train, his grey Anthony Eden hat perched at a jaunty angle on the side of his head, in fits of laughter, having had the night of his life with the police.

He had been quite amazed when they put him into the Black Maria. Because of his attendance at the House of Lords he was carrying his largest, most powerful hearing aid which was built into a dispatch case. As soon as they settled into the Black Maria he tried to reach out for his dispatch case but his arm was immediately grasped again. I suppose they were afraid he would try to attack them with whatever was in the case. They arrived at the Police Station and he was marched in to give his statement (to him his offence still unknown because he had not heard a word). Once he explained he was stone deaf and must have his aid he got on better. Asked for his name, he said,

"The Duke of Montrose."

A cynical smile crossed the face of the young policeman.

"Come on, now, don't try that one on us, it will be the King of England next, I suppose. Where have you come from?"

"Brodick Castle, Isle of Arran," he replied.

"Now then, now then, you just think again. What have you got to prove it?"

Father at the General Assembly of the Church of Scotland, Edinburgh

Father did a quick search of his pockets and pulled out a piece of headed notepaper which only led to further suspicion as on it was engraved 'Buchanan Castle, Drymen, Glasgow', but at least it had a ducal coronet at the top.

He explained he had been at the House of Lords all day. Unfortunately when they telephoned the House for confirmation whoever they spoke to said the Duke of Montrose had not been there.

It took Father a very long time to discover that the police had already checked with the hotel at Euston and found he had signed in as 'James Graham, Auchmar, Drymen'. Father then had to give the police a complete explanation of the title system of Great Britain. His family name was Graham, his title was Duke of Montrose. Scotland, at that time, was only entitled to elect 16 peers a year to sit in the House of Lords. Most of the peers have English titles as well which enables them to sit in the House, and his English title was Earl Belford which he had used in the House that afternoon, hence when they phoned the House of Lords the police were told the Duke of Montrose had not signed in. In the end they believed that he had travelled from Arran and that he did live at Auchmar, Drymen, and no longer at Buchanan Castle.

Then they questioned him about the cases, all with different initials on them and different names on the labels. He knew one was Mother's and one was mine, but he could not remember the maid's surname, the chauffeur he knew as Tommy, but could not remember his second name. The police explained that from the luggage van he had collected a case belonging to a doctor who had come all the way to London to lecture about an operation. Father always maintained that a torso was in the case but I really think the surgeon's tools of his trade were the contents. However, the operation could not go ahead. They had found the case Father should have had under his First Class sleeper bunk and this was returned to him. How he enjoyed the episode!

In the Spring of 1935 His Royal Highness The Duke of York came to stay three nights at Auchmar while carrying out some official engagements in Glasgow and the Clyde. He arrived tired after a busy day and we had a peaceful evening. The following morning he left for Glasgow and Mother and Father were invited to lunch with His Royal Highness by the Lord Provost of Glasgow and then proceed to a Football Cup game. It was arranged, rather on the spur of the moment, that Mother would leave for home in our Studebaker and the Lord Provost would bring the rest of the party out to join a cocktail party after the game finished.

Somehow no-one thought to tell the police of the new arrangements. Mother slipped out of the Royal Box and left the stadium and got into the car driven by old Tommy Watson. They were shocked to find that a police car swung out in front of them, all sirens blazing, clearing the traffic as they went. The horrible truth dawned that Mother had taken His Royal Highness's escort! In true Hollywood jargon she shouted, "Follow that car!" and old Tommy, clutching the wheel, did credit to Starsky and Hutch all through the centre of Glasgow! Mother waved her handkerchief out of the window, giving the 'slow down' sign, but the police obviously thought they were being pressed into more daring action and went faster.

T.R.H. The Duke & Duchess of York

It was not until they were clear of the outskirts of Glasgow that the police became uneasy at my mother's behaviour and stopped. The police were shocked and asked why they had behaved so stupidly. If only they had pulled up at the side of the road the police would have had to stop as well. Now they were pressed for time to get back to the stadium in time for the Duke of York.

That evening, among other guests for dinner, was the Rev. Mr. Lacey, our minister at Buchanan. His great interest, and indeed work, that occupied some years was to get the County Council to build public lavatories at Balmaha. Evidently he sat next to His Royal Highness after dinner and over a glass of port told him of his big fight with the Council, told of their arguments, enlarged on the subject, and waxed eloquent. As we went up to our rooms at night the Duke said,

"Whatever I know or don't know about Great Britain, at least I know all about the lavatories at Balmaha!"

The following morning was free of engagements and His Royal Highness wanted to go for a walk, so Mother and I took him a little way towards the foot of the Conic Hill. First of all I saw a sheep stranded on its back among some gorse bushes. Always impetuous, I drew attention to it, tried to lift it and carry it where the shepherd was likely to see it. The Duke took it from me and carried it. As I passed Mother I heard her, in a low voice, say,

"I wish to goodness you would keep your mouth shut."

It was a pity she took that attitude as I think we were both enjoying ourselves. However, worse was to come. I suggested that all the gorse bushes should be burnt as it was a good day for burning, and that I knew Father intended they should be burnt as he had told me to do it. This the Duke thought would be enormous fun and struck a match. In moments we were nearly surrounded by flames. At that moment the worried face of the detective peered over the top of the bushes. Apparently we had been followed through the walk. When he could not stand the responsibility any longer he came and suggested we should withdraw, which we did, and left the fire to burn itself out.

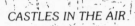

18

SCHOOL DAYS

HEN I was 13 it was decided that I should be sent to Glasgow for fencing lessons at M. Croisier's School, and I simply loved this. I must have been reasonably good at it because it was not long after the commencement of lessons that old M.Croisier handed me over to be taught by his son, Pierre, and several other of his pupils were brought in to fence with me. I was, absolutely delighted when he said that he would like to have me in for a second lesson each week as he thought I might be good enough to join some team that he was getting up. When I got home I was starry-eyed about this opportunity, and to this day I have no idea why the news was received so badly by Mother. Whether she was alarmed by the fact that a good-looking young Frenchman was now my tutor, or whether she visualised the team boarding a bus (which she always called a "charabanc") and disappearing into the night like a football team with coloured lavatory paper streaming from the windows and coloured tartan toories on our heads, I have no idea, but I was never allowed back there again. Instead, I was sent to some drab musical school to learn how to sing which was stupid in the extreme as to this day I cannot sing "God Save the Queen" in tune!

Coming back to Buchanan from my lessons across the Stockiemuir road from Glasgow it was a joy to stop for a moment at what is now known as "The Queen's View". From there the ground slopes down towards Loch Lomond, and in winter the russet reds with heather and bracken growing in the sun, down to the richly wooded land and the farms that were at that time Buchanan Estate. The loch, stood like a blue gem dotted with wooded islands and all that you can see on the right hand side of Loch Lomond, including Ben Lomond, was all part of the old estate, a breathtaking view indeed.

It was decided I should be sent to school the following autumn. Getting school uniforms and the inevitable traumatic effect of packing up a school trunk and checking things off the list filled me with dismay. My mother accompanied me to London and saw me onto the school train for Southover Manor, Lewes, Sussex. There seemed to be hundreds of girls, all dressed in brown. The only face I knew was Susan Ridley whom I had not seen since the days of riding in the goat trap at Brodick when she was pitched head first into the rhododendron bushes.

I don't remember being particularly upset by sleeping in a dormitory or being taught in a class, but having been in the company of grown-ups all my life, and having had very few playmates I found it extremely difficult to make friends with the girls of my age at first, though after two years at school I came away with my fair share of friends.

After that I went to a finishing school, Brilliantmont, Lausanne, where we learnt domestic science in French. This I found enormous fun. There were a certain number of British girls there in the three different colleges but also girls from most countries in the world.

I don't know that we really learnt a lot because our French was fairly shaky, and if in the laundry class, or the cooking class, or any of the other classes the teacher shouted at one, one simply changed what one was doing and did it some other way, and if she shut up we reckoned we were all right. I loved the freedom there and being able to go down into town when we were allowed out in the company of another girl.

For some reason I was crazy about all the different cheeses that one could buy in Switzerland, although I did not know one from the other; but after every visit to the town I would come back with two or three different kinds. On one occasion I had bought a most ghastly, strong-smelling goats' cheese which smelt worse than any midden on a good old Scottish farm. It obviously could not be kept in the bedroom which I shared with another girl or we would have been gassed, so after a certain consultation with the various other girls who came into my cheese party we decided to put it down the lavatory. We flushed the plug and all seemed well until the next morning when I found the housekeeper with a group of plumbers ripping up the lavatory system. The cheese had been found somewhere trapped in the system, and although everybody was asked where it had originated, thank goodness nobody gave me away, and I certainly was not man enough to admit. Even after this there must have been quite a few crumbs of cheese left around on the dressing table, because at night my companion, Alison, and I were woken up with the most extraordinary sound coming from the waste paper basket, and on putting the light on we found a mouse trapped in a hairnet bouncing round the floor in circles. We had to spend a considerable time getting it out of the hairnet, and then we didn't know what to do with it so we let it go in the passage.

Our weekends were spent on various expeditions skiing in winter, or hiking in summer, in the Mont Blanc area. One's memory of summer is of carpets of the most glorious wild flowers wherever one looked. I think my French must have been average, but the school decided I should have extra tuition, and for a long time I was grateful to them because in the evening they sent me to an old retired actress.

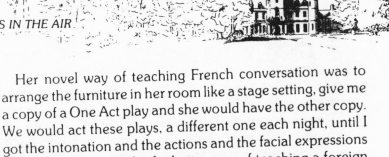

Her novel way of teaching French conversation was to arrange the furniture in her room like a stage setting, give me a copy of a One Act play and she would have the other copy. We would act these plays, a different one each night, until I got the intonation and the actions and the facial expressions correct. I cannot think of a better way of teaching a foreign language because all nationalities are recognisable by their gestures and facial expressions.

I was saddened when my parents decided that another friend from Brilliantmont and myself should go to live some months in France with a French family. I think the idea was that we spoke too much English at Brilliantmont, and if we were sent to live with a family we would have no opportunity, which was not quite correct as Jane and I chattered in our room in English all that time.

The old chateau we lived in was near Blois on the river Loire. We spent a lot of time going on expeditions round the famous chateaux of the Loire, but also met a lot of French people, friends of the family. On one occasion Mme Charles, the daughter of the house, drove Jane and myself to stay in a frightfully smart and large chateau by the name of Chateau de Villegougis. The owners appeared to young teenagers such as ourselves to be quite shatteringly smart with all their clothes obviously made for them by the most fashionable houses in Paris. As all British teenagers who had not been round the world very much, we were speechless.

Jane and I were put into bedrooms at the opposite ends of the largest corridor you could imagine and each supplied with a ladies maid. On these occasions one always blushes, knowing that one's clothes aren't nearly smart enough to be unpacked by someone else's ladies maid. We were so shy we wouldn't have been able to tell you our names in English, let alone a conversation with a French ladies maid in the local vernacular .We soon discovered that we were not to be allowed to wear our own dressing gowns. The maid put us into a *robe de bain*, then, carrying our sponge bags and our towels preceded us to our bathrooms. It so happened that Jane, with her maid, came out of her bedroom at one end of the passage at the same moment that I came out of my bedroom with my maid at the other end, and for some reason it had been decided that we were to go to the bathroom at the opposite ends of our corridor. Our little processions marched towards each other and passed each other without a word, we were so near to giggles!

My bathroom was in a room with clothes rails like a shop, covered with the Comptess's clothes. In the middle of the room was a bath. The maid had a thermometer bobbing about like a cork in the water, asking me what temperature I liked my bath. I, of course, had no idea in Fahrenheit, let alone in Centigrade! After this traumatic experience we dressed in our best clothes which, frankly, with the smart company we were keeping, looked as if we had bought them at a second hand shop.

All too soon the moment arrived when we were ushered down to dinner where there was a large assembly of people. After the pre-dinner drinks which the grown-ups had, although I didn't, we went into the dining room which could be better described as a banqueting hall. I suppose the dinner party was for about 30 people, the table covered with a white linen damask cloth and beside each plate was a row of glasses, I suppose about five at each setting. True to the French habit of not having a different knife and fork for each course, there was a stand to put your knife and fork beside each plate, which again was new to me.

When the first course came round I hesitated and looked round the table for the salt cellar, and the host asked what I

Chateau de Villegougis

was looking for. Stupidly I said "the salt", whereupon the footman was called, and the conversation ceased while the footman was dispatched to get salt from the kitchen. There could be no worse insult to the chef than somebody wanting to put salt on his concoctions. The whole dinner party was held up for quite some time until the footman arrived back with a saucer of salt on a silver salver, and a teaspoon. Of course, long before its arrival I had realised what a terrible *faux pas* I had made, but there was nothing I could do except to remember for the rest of my life never to look for salt and pepper at anybody's dinner table ever again.

The reason for the party was a stag hunt the following day given by a neighbour in honour of the most beautiful Spanish woman, wife of some important *Grandee* who was paying a visit to France.

She was mounted on a fine chestnut horse, dressed in a

long, flowing sapphire blue habit as one only sees depicted in old paintings, the habit flowing to the horse's knees. On her head she wore a little tricorn hat around which was a diaphanous scarf of white floating out behind her as she rode away from the meet. She looked as though she had just newly walked out of history, and I thought she was the most beautiful woman I had ever seen.

Being accustomed to the quick, humane death of deer when they are stalked properly in Scotland, hunting deer as they did here nauseated me; but the ceremony that went with a large ceremonial hunt was picturesque. All the foresters were dressed in the uniform of the family who were giving the hunt — velvet caps, long green jackets with gold bands on the sleeves and pockets, green breeches and long boots. They carried big brass French hunting horns over their shoulders. The entire hunt, hounds and hunt servants assembled in the courtyard of the castle, and some hundreds of people came for the day. When all were assembled the hunting horns played certain calls before they rode away into the forest. We followed in the car with Mme. Charles, though we did not see a lot of the hunt. In the evening after a buffet supper we assembled at the top of the balustraded staircase leading from the hall to the courtyard. In the courtyard were assembled the estate workers with flares at the end of long shafts which they held, forming a semi-circle of firelight. The hounds were in the centre of this circle and the stag that had been killed lay there on a mat of fir branches while the horns sounded *la Mort*, a hunting call for the death of a stag. The Spanish lady, standing at the top of the stairs in the place of honour next to the host was praised in speeches and replied, giving her thanks, and she was then presented with the trophy head of the stag. To my utter amazement I was then called forth, which perhaps was the most embarrassing

191

moment of the whole visit, and presented with the slot (hoof). I don't remember making any speech in reply, I don't think I did, I just scuttled back amongst the crowd of guests.

19

THE LIGHT BEFORE THE STORM

HE years 1937 and 1938 were depressing. War was the talk wherever we went and with whoever we met — war — Hitler — Germany — on and on it went.

In the autumn of 1938 the Gaelic Mod was held in Glasgow and Mother and Father, with the Bannermans, Tiny and myself, attended, as Mother did each year, but the political situation hung like a cloud over our heads. Everybody was talking about war and the Prime Minister's proposed visit to Germany. I remember, most graphically, that, during the middle of a ceilidh in the Grand Hotel at Charing Cross late at night, John Bannerman came into the lounge waving the latest edition of the evening papers showing photographs of Mr. Chamberlain arriving back in Britain by air, and large headlines saying "PEACE IN OUR TIME". A tremendous cheer went up and there was a completely different tempo in the crowd.

Tiny had come to Scotland to join me, and together we went to the Skye Gathering at Portree. What fun we had making new friends together! We did the rounds of the Highland Balls — Oban, Aboyne, then Inverness. The fears of war were gathering all the time, and during the Inverness Ball all naval officers were called out to rejoin their ships. Naturally the officers of the other services felt they should go as well. It was a dismal affair.

Shortly after Christmas, after Tiny had returned home, Father took John and Ray Bannerman, Mother and myself out to Trinidad where my beloved father had invested more of the family fortunes in an oil well called Seperia. On his previous visit to Port of Spain the year before, he had made the acquaintance, in a rather unusual manner, of a man called McBride. On this first visit, when the ship tied up alongside the docks at Port of Spain, he noticed a man of small stature standing beside two Rolls Royce cars. He came on board and introduced himself to Father as a cousin of John McBride who leased out rowing boats and bathing boxes on the sandy beach at Brodick. To Father's astonishment, he offered him the use of one of the Rolls Royce cars for the duration of his visit, and told him how he had come to be in Trinidad.

The name McBride, in Port of Spain, was illustrious indeed. As a lad, he had left Arran and joined a merchant sailing ship going to the West Indies. When they arrived at Port of Spain he noticed that ships had to stand nearly a mile offshore and could off-load their cargoes only at high tide when the barges could reach dry land over a vast expanse of mud and sand. He jumped ship and began to construct wooden jetties such as he had seen in Brodick, which enabled the barges to work either side of high tide, for which facility he charged pier dues.

From this small and simple start he expanded slowly and surely, eventually buying the foreshore of Port of Spain where he built docks, dry docks and warehouses. By this time he was so successful that he also bought a valley beyond the mountains near Port of Spain and farmed citrus fruits, which led to his building a fruit juice bottling factory.

Our trip, unfortunately, was to visit a less successful venture. Having sailed out in a German ship, stopping off at Barbados for a week, we found things were not running according to plan when we arrived in Port of Spain. It was perfectly obvious that a very large sum of money was going down the drain. My father had engaged a manager to run the mine, and on our arrival my parents were upset when we visited the manager's flat. We saw the most gorgeous lady, wearing a large white hat and white dress (of the sort photographed in the centre pages of *Vogue* rather than at the beginning or the end)! From her ears dangled long jade earrings. We discovered that she was the hostess. I was quite fascinated by her, but Mother took every precaution that I had no opportunity to speak to her and there was always a hush when her name was mentioned!

Having stayed there for a week or two, we visited Tobago for a short period. Father arranged that we should sail home once again in a German ship, while he continued on his own to America where he had some business to attend to.

The "Peace In Our Time" was already beginning to wear extremely thin, but we had no reason for concern when we started from Trinidad. During the daytime we enjoyed the beautiful ship with its ample space to roam around, the swimming pool, deck chairs and the deck games. Within the first two or three days of sailing in the Atlantic, however, we discovered that after dinner the passengers were debarred from going on the main deck and the upper deck. Somehow or other John Bannerman and I went onto the deck and peeped up onto the top deck where we saw the ship's doctor in full S.S. uniform, drilling the entire crew! The canvas covers had been removed from various objects on deck which were, in fact, guns. We were sailing in an armed merchantman!

Outside the Purser's Office stood two tickertape machines. One was printing German messages, and reeled off screeds of news, but the other one, which printed English only, showed a small paragraph or two of world news. We tried to get some of the German passengers to translate what

what was being said in their news, but no-one was willing to oblige.

After a day or two there was one sentence in English — "Czechoslovakia is now Germany". It was quite clear that the screed of German news had been telling of troop movements.

My mother asked the Captain what would happen if war was declared. He told her that in the previous October his orders had been to impound the ship and the passengers, at Montevideo. Now his orders were sealed and he couldn't tell us, but he imagined the same would apply. It could hardly have been described as the ultimate in sunshine holidays! We were very thankful when we arrived and disembarked at Southampton.

Having gone through Customs, we bought a paper before boarding the train, and there, in large letters, was the heading "LOST PRINCESS". On reading further we discovered it was my beloved Tiny who, due to a family row, had run away from their Paris house and was thought to be in England.

We knew at once that she would be looking for Mother, and had not known that we were still abroad. We also knew that she was very friendly with all the Wimbledon tennis players, who trained out in Monte Carlo during the winter.

When we got to London we telephoned Bunny Austin to see if he knew her whereabouts, and he put us in touch with one of the women tennis players. Through her we eventually got in touch with Tiny, who had run away in the clothes she stood up in, with practically no money to keep herself. She had booked into a hotel where breakfast was included in the price so that at least she got one meal a day. Once she found her friends she was all right, and we took her back to Arran with us.

That year, I was to "Come out" in the London Season, and be presented at Court. Most girls would have been very thrilled at the prospect, but I did not know enough young people to really look forward to the parties, being as gauche as I was. I was allowed no make-up, no smoking and no drinking. I still had long hair, and I didn't have too good a figure. However, Mother arranged that we should go to the house of her friend, Mrs. Wynn Finch, in Wilton Crescent, for the spring and summer.

Our first visit was to get me clothed. Mother had the idea that debutantes should be dressed in pastel shades and very 'little girly' fashions. My idea was different. The first dress I fell in love with was flame chiffon, low cut at the front and back, with a huge permanently pleated skirt. This was not allowed. The second dress was clinging black satin — you can guess the answer. Thirdly, I spied a dress of dark sapphire net banded in satin, with an overblown silk rose at the waist. This was allowed — provided the rose was lifted to hide any cleavage. I was then taken to *Worth* in Grosvenor Street and, as we walked through the door, facing us at the foot of the staircase was a model draping herself over the banister, in a diaphanous pale grey concoction with a flesh-coloured underslip which gave the impression that she had nothing on. Goodness! Teenagers can be difficult! This was, I thought, just the dress for me — and it was the pale pastel colour that Mother wanted. I argued as hard as I could till I was removed from *Worth*!

We searched London for what Mother described as 'sensible dresses'. Eventually she got her way. Both parents were so out of touch with modern society they did not realize how things had changed since their young day.

The first ball I was taken to was given by Lady Astor. Everyone, except ourselves, had made up dinner parties, and arrived in groups of twenty or thirty. We arrived — just Father, Mother and myself. I knew no-one and they knew

Princess Antoinette of Monaco (Tiny)

only a handful of people. That evening was the worst. After that they managed to get me asked to join dinner parties.

Frankly, I never enjoyed the dances, but I loved our Ascot party, the Richmond Horse Show, the Royal Tattoo and the Saturdays at Hurlingham to watch the polo matches, and by the end of the season I had made a lot of friends.

I was presented at Court dressed in the palest pink dress, which was entirely encrusted in minute beads, which gave it a shimmering effect, long, white, elbow-length kid gloves, and carrying the pink ostrich feather fan that Sir Abe Baillie had given me when I was out in South Africa, now mounted with a mother-of-pearl handle. My hair was dressed with three curled ostrich feathers, as was the mode.

We joined a queue of cars in the Mall, which was lined with

Myself on my 21st birthday

people pressing against the window. My excitement grew till we arrived at the side door of Buckingham Palace and were ushered up to the assembly point. Eventually the doors opened and the Royal Family took their places on the dias.

Mother and I were called after the Duchess of Marlborough and her daughter. Mother curtsied first, and I followed. There is always a danger of catching one's heel in the dress and over-balancing. It seldom happens, but it is a nightmare thought that haunts one's mind! After being presented, we were shown to chairs in the Throne Room and could watch the other girls make the curtsey.

The following week we were invited to a Court Ball given in honour of Princess Olga, sister of Princess Marina, Duchess of Kent. I really enjoyed this magnificent ball. Against the background of the gold and white room, the jewels were stunning. The beautiful dresses and the scarlet uniforms of the men all added to the sparkle. To complete my joy, I think I danced every dance. This was, without doubt, the climax of my London season.

We returned north to Brodick, having made arrangements for the friends I had made to come and stay to shoot and stalk. However, the thunders of war were rumbling louder. We received a telegram from Hugh Trenchard, son of the Marshal of the R.A.F.: "Unable to keep my shooting date at Brodick due to a possible invitation to shoot a larger quarry". That spoke for all the young men I met in the London season.

It was the end of a way of life. When war was declared, Father offered Buchanan Castle to the Red Cross, for the rehabilitation of the wounded. They could have walked in with little alteration. Instead, he found by accident a large gathering from the Ministry of Health, who informed him they were commandeering it to make a thousand-bedded hospital. They started cutting trees and terracing the garden

Ronald, Father and Angus, all RNVR. This picture was taken during World War II, when Angus was in command of HMS Ludlow.

201

before any agreement had been signed. John Bannerman, the Factor, had already joined the Air Ministry and so was not available to see to the business side of the takeover. For example there was no agreement as to what was to happen to the sewage plant when Buchanan was handed back; this meant that when my Father died in 1954 my brother had to pay the local authorities £30,000 to take over the plant. I won't bore you with more, but Buchanan is now a ruin with trees growing out of the lovely public reception rooms.

In Arran life changed too. Lamlash became a Naval base, with HMS Cardiff the Gunnery Training Ship based there. Also, convoy escorts assembled in the bay before the Atlantic crossing. When the Commandos were first formed there were 8,000 men billeted in Arran, including eight at the Castle.

Nanny died in 1942. Worried as she was about my two brothers who were in the RNVR, and my sister living in London and nursing in First-Aid posts, Nanny found comfort by the company of some of the Commandos who used to visit her and read to her, a kindness she talked of often. With her death, part of our lives went with her. I can hear her voice saying, "I've seen the day, and now the day sees me!" We never really knew what it meant, but it sounded like wisdom the way she said it.

I spent the war at Bletchley Park working with Enigma, having failed to get into the services due to my history of tuberculosis. At the end of the war I did not admit to tuberculosis, and sailed to India on a troop ship as a Welfare Officer in the Red Cross. My health gave way and I felt guilty. For more than twenty years I tried to make amends, and became President of the Arran branch of the Red Cross, Chairman of the Red Cross Subcommittee for the Care of the Young Disabled, member of Council, and a

member of the Executive Committee, which meant I travelled to the mainland about three times a fortnight for all those years through gales and tranquil seas.

I look back in happiness that I was so lucky as to share the good times, but I often weep in my heart for the security of the days long gone – for you, Nanny. I weep for the rustle of your long grey skirts, for your little black laced boots, the smell of mushrooms cooking on the nursery fire, for winkles in the brown enamelled pot cooking for tea on the Dougarie shore; for your stately progress beside Nanny Wanstall and the laughter with Tiny and Rainier, and even for your scoldings.

Not for you stranger for many years,
    am I crying,
Though I loved you, my tears
    are not for your dying.
With a pang does memory surrender
    from its great store,
The vest on the nursery fender,
    the light under the door,
The petersham belt creaking,
    the alpaca silhouette,
The slow voice speaking
    comfort. Yet and yet....
Dear as you were, I am reconciled
    to your long sleep.
But for Virginia as a child
    I weep, Nanny, I weep.

Virginia Graham

Yes, Nanny, I weep.